Copyright © 2009 by Quirk Productions, Inc.

All rights reserved. No part of this book may be reproduced in any form without written permission from the publisher.

Library of Congress Cataloging in Publication Number: 2009922638

ISBN: 978-1-59474-261-3

Printed in China

Typeset in ITC Century

Designed by Bryn Ashburn and Jenny Kraemer
Illustrations by Jesse Ewing
Edited by Sarah O'Brien
Production management by Melissa Jacobson

Distributed in North America by Chronicle Books
680 Second Street
San Francisco, CA 94107

10 9 8 7 6 5 4 3 2 1

Quirk Books
215 Church Street
Philadelphia, PA 19106
www.irreference.com
www.quirkbooks.com

WINE SECRETS

ADVICE FROM WINEMAKERS, SOMMELIERS, AND CONNOISSEURS

BY MARNIE OLD

QUIRK BOOKS

PHILADELPHIA

Table of Contents

Introduction.. 8

CHAPTER 1: WINE BASICS   10

Winemaking: How Sweet Grape Juice Becomes Dry Wine...................... 12
Ed Sbragia, Winemaker

White vs. Red Wine: Differences Run More Than Skin Deep 17
Gina Gallo, Winemaker

Grape Varieties: One Grape Species, Many Varietals........................... 20
Michael Mondavi, Vintner

Sunshine and Wine Style: How Climate Affects Body and Flavor 23
Laura Maniec, Master Sommelier

Terroir, or the "Taste of the Place": Why Region Matters in Wine 28
Jean-Luc Le Dû, Sommelier and Wine Retailer

Understanding Oak: The Role of Barrels in Winemaking 32
Tom Stevenson, Wine Author

Old World/New World: Differences in Philosophy and Flavor 36
Randall Grahm, Winemaker

CHAPTER 2: WINE TASTING   42

How to Taste Wine Like a Pro 44
Richard Betts, Master Sommelier and Winemaker

How to Find Words for Wine's Elusive Aromas............................... 49
Ann Noble, Wine Educator

How to Determine Whether a Wine Is Dry 53
Jean Trimbach, Vintner

How to Detect and Make Sense of Acidity in Wine 57
Michael Weiss, Wine Educator

How to Assess Body in Wine (and Why It Matters) 61
David Ramey, Winemaker

IIow to Get a Grip on Tannin in Red Wines 65
Zelma Long, Winemaker

How to Judge Whether a Wine Is "Good" 69
Traci Dutton, Sommelier and Wine Educator

CHAPTER 3: WINE SHOPPING   **72**

How to Get Started in Wine Stores 74
Madeline Triffon, Master Sommelier

How to Relate to Your Wine Retailer. 77
Robert Kacher, Wine Importer

How to Guesstimate Wine Style from Packaging Clues 81
Olivia Boru, Sommelier

How to Decide Which Wines Are Ready to Drink 86
Jancis Robinson, Master of Wine and Wine Author

How to Compare Corks and Screw Caps, Bottles and Boxes 90
Melissa Monosoff, Sommelier

How to Find Values by Stepping Off the Beaten Track. 94
Ron Edwards, Master Sommelier

How to Find the Best Wines by Sticking to the Classics. 98
Kevin Zraly, Wine Educator and Author

CHAPTER 4: WINE AND FOOD PAIRING   **102**

How to Get Started Pairing Wine and Food 104
Evan Goldstein, Master Sommelier

How to Pair More Gracefully by Choosing Light-Bodied Wines. 108
Terry Theise, Wine Importer

How to Find Delicious Combinations by "Matching" Colors 112
Fred Dexheimer, Master Sommelier

How to Understand *Umami*—The Famous "Fifth Taste" 117
Doug Frost, Master of Wine and Master Sommelier

How to Pair Wine with Challenging Vegetables 121
Natalie MacLean, Wine Author

How to Choose Wines for Foods with a Spicy Kick 125
Guy Stout, Master Sommelier

How to Pair with Sweet Dessert Wines. 128
Donald Ziraldo, Vintner and Wine Author

CHAPTER 5: WINE IN RESTAURANTS   **132**

How to Gauge a Restaurant's Wine Savvy 134
Mark Oldman, Wine Author

How to Act Like You Know What You're Doing When Ordering Wine. 139
Fred Dame, Master Sommelier

How to Get the Best Wine Advice in Restaurants 144
Larry Stone, Master Sommelier

How to Pick Wines for Multicourse Meals 148
Randy Caparoso, Sommelier

How to Choose Wines for a Large Party 152
Christie Dufault, Sommelier

How, When, and Why to Send Back a Bottle of Wine 156
Piero Selvaggio, Restaurateur

CHAPTER 6: WINE AT HOME   **160**

How to Preserve Open Wine (Yes, You Can Freeze It) 162
Ronn Wiegand, Master of Wine and Master Sommelier

How to Serve and Store Wine at the Right Temperature. 166
Mark Squires, Wine Writer

How to Choose an All-Purpose Wineglass 170
Tara Q. Thomas, Wine Author

How to Use Leftover Wine in the Kitchen 174
Jacques Pépin, Chef

How to Safely Open a Bottle of Champagne 177
Charles Curtis, Master of Wine

How to Get a Handle on Mature Wines.................................... 181
Michael Martini, Winemaker

Index... 186
Acknowledgments... 190
About the Author... 191

Introduction

THIS BOOK IS A COLLECTION OF PEARLS OF WINE WISDOM FROM FORTY LEADING FIGURES IN THE WINE WORLD. THESE SIMPLE TIPS AREN'T RECOMMENDATIONS OR traditional lessons about styles or regions. Rather, they're useful insights and practical hints designed with the everyday wine drinker in mind. Inside, you'll find everything from basic concepts that help untangle wine's complexity to specific advice on which features are important in an all-purpose wineglass.

As wine professionals, the experts cited on these pages have all built their lives around one of life's purest pleasures. Like works of art, the best wines can transport us with a single sip to another place and time. The extraordinary properties of wine have been recognized for centuries. Even the simplest ones are refreshing, delicious, and nutritious and can melt away the anxieties of the day.

Yet, there's no question that wine can also be a source of frustration. Compared to virtually every other food or beverage, wine seems fraught with hazards. Impenetrable labels, pairing rules, serving temperatures—newcomers are confronted with an overwhelming number of choices and service rituals that can stand in the way of appreciating what's in the bottle.

An entire industry has sprung up to support wine as an elite beverage, building a world in which what you know about wine is a reflection of your social status. But, that's not what wine is really about. Socrates had it right:

The more you know, the more you know you don't know. And, with wine, that's okay. The minutia that gets all the attention—vintages, winemaking techniques, soil types, individual wine reviews—isn't what most wine drinkers need to know. What's important is to learn just enough about wine to help you take more pleasure from drinking it—how to describe what you like, how its flavors shift with food, and so on.

Those who know the most about wine tend to have the fewest pretensions. Sommeliers and winemakers don't put wine on a pedestal; we invite it into our lives. We know that wine isn't a "liquid asset" to be hoarded and traded; it's a liquid pleasure to be shared and enjoyed. People who know wine in their bones rarely stand on ceremony, and their expertise brings a measure of common sense to bear that dispels snobbery.

In my work as a sommelier and a wine educator, I meet a lot of people who are worried about picking the wrong wine or serving it incorrectly. If we allow wine to induce stress, we've really got ourselves turned around. The idea is to be drinking wine to *relieve* stress. That's why I wrote this book. I wanted to share with wine drinkers everywhere the kinds of ideas that help instill the confidence and calm that experts feel and banish the fearfulness and stress experienced by beginners.

CHAPTER
ONE

Wine Basics

WINE IS TRULY SPECIAL, CAPABLE OF GIVING GREAT PLEASURE. IT IS HEALTHFUL AND DELICIOUS, RELAXING AND NUTRITIOUS. WHAT'S NOT TO LIKE? YET, WINE can be equally frustrating. No other agricultural product is as impenetrably labeled; centuries of elite status have left us subject to arcane hierarchies and confusing legal terminology. Attempting to navigate the sea of wine options can leave the novice feeling powerless, perhaps even paralyzed with self-doubt. Little wonder that most people prefer to buy wines based on third-party endorsements or recommendations rather than choosing for themselves.

Knowledge is power. Upon discovering wine's joys, our first instinct is to learn as much as we can, to master wine through sheer memorization. But wine is far too complex for this strategy to be successful. Most wine books and classes focus so tightly on technical data—such as appellations and grape varietals, soil types and vinification techniques—that beginners end up missing the forest for the trees.

As a wine educator, I usually recommend the opposite approach. Rather than learn what sets each style apart, let's begin with what they all share. Wine is much easier to understand once you've been introduced to a few key concepts. In this section, you'll find a short list of useful generalizations; these "big picture" ideas will help illustrate how the wine world works.

WINEMAKING:

HOW SWEET GRAPE JUICE BECOMES DRY WINE

———◆•••◆———

ED SBRAGIA
Winemaker

WINE IS MADE from grapes—specifically, fermented grapes. During fermentation sugar is consumed by microorganisms called yeasts and converted into alcohol. Because yeasts are everywhere, fermentation happens all the time throughout nature. Anything sugary can ferment; in fact, it's an early phase of spoilage. Have you ever taken a trip and forgotten to clean out the fridge first? If the orange juice tasted sour and fizzy when you came home, congratulations: You made orange wine.

There is no need to master chemical formulas to appreciate wine. But if you want to get a handle on how the wine world works, a basic grasp of fermentation is a good place to start.

- **IN WINEMAKING, THE MAIN PROCESS THAT OCCURS IS FERMENTATION, IN WHICH YEASTS CONSUME SUGAR AND GENERATE ALCOHOL.**
Any sweet liquid can ferment, and all beverage alcohol is made via fermentation. Beer and sake are fermented beverages too, but they are based on malted barley and moldy rice instead of ripe grapes. When yeasts metabolize sugar, they break it down into alcohol and

ED SBRAGIA is one of California's most respected winemakers. He holds the title of winemaster emeritus at Napa Valley's Beringer Vineyards in honor of his 32-year tenure at California's oldest continuously operating winery. His wines have garnered countless awards, and he was instrumental in developing Beringer's legendary Private Reserve program. Although Sbragia continues to consult for Beringer, he has recently focused on his own family's vineyard land in Sonoma County's Dry Creek valley. In 2004 he launched Sbragia Family Vineyards, where he and his son Adam make wine together.

carbon dioxide. Sometimes we preserve some natural carbonation, but for most wines we allow the carbon dioxide bubbles to escape.

- **MICROSCOPIC YEASTS ARE WHAT MAKE WINEMAKING TICK; THEY ARE THE KEY TO FRUIT'S MIRACULOUS TRANSFORMATION INTO WINE.**
Yeasts are living things—single-celled members of the fungus family. As with any other life form, yeasts are hard-wired to eat and reproduce. They eat sugar, which provides the energy they need to reproduce, starting the cycle over again. Ironically, yeasts' own byproduct eventually becomes toxic for them; they cannot survive once wine reaches 15 to 16 percent alcohol.

- **GRAPES ARE IDEALLY SUITED FOR WINEMAKING BECAUSE THEY ARE SWEET, FLAVORFUL, AND JUICY.**
Sweeter than most other fruits, grapes are rich in highly fermentable glucose and fructose, which makes them able to produce high-alcohol wine. Historically, people chose to ferment grapes rather than, say, strawberries because grapes made stronger wine. High alcohol was desirable because it is nutritious, resists spoilage, and intensifies flavor.

- **GRAPE JUICE MAY BE SUGARY, BUT MOST WINES ARE DRY, A WINE TERM MEANING "NOT PERCEPTIBLY SWEET."**
During winemaking, yeasts break down sugar. The process slows and stops naturally when no sugar remains, similar to a car running out of gas. Juice that started off extremely sweet—with 20 percent sugar content or higher—ends up with so little (generally less than 1 percent) that the tongue is unable to perceive it. We call this state *dryness*, which sounds confusing but really just means the absence of sweetness. It is sometimes expressed as a measurement of the leftover, or residual, sugar quantified in either grams per liter or as a percentage by weight.

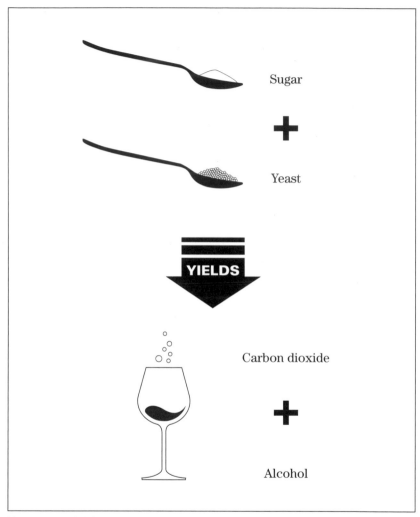

Sugar

+

Yeast

YIELDS

Carbon dioxide

+

Alcohol

*Beverage alcohol is created through **fermentation**—the action of yeast organisms that converts sugar into alcohol and carbon dioxide.*

- **MANY FACTORS INFLUENCE OUR PERCEPTION OF A WINE'S SWEETNESS OR DRYNESS.**

  Our senses are not lab instruments; they are strongly influenced by context. Two wines may have identical sugar content but be perceived as differing in sweetness. For example, sweetness in wine can be balanced or even completely masked by high levels of acidity, bitterness, or carbonation. Elevated alcohol, on the other hand, can dramatically boost perceived sweetness. Also, some sugars taste sweeter than others; of the two types abundant in grapes, fructose seems twice as sweet as glucose.

  In addition, we tend to associate certain sensations with others, which can lead us to imagine a sweet taste in wines that smell reminiscent of sugary things. Everything else being equal, a wine that smells like raisins will likely seem sweeter than a wine that smells like lemon peel.

- **THE VAST MAJORITY OF WINES ARE DRY, BUT THERE ARE EXCEPTIONS THAT RANGE FROM FAINTLY SWEET TO STICKY-CANDY SWEET.**

  Centuries ago, winemakers made their wines dry for practical reasons: to maximize alcoholic strength and avert spoilage. However, a little sweetness is definitely pleasant in some wine styles. Winemakers worldwide have devised techniques for retaining some sugar and rendering sweet wines more stable, such as interrupting fermentation before it's complete or concentrating the grapes beforehand. The simplest way is to make a dry wine first and then blend in a little stabilized juice or juice concentrate. The result is a pleasingly sweet wine.

- **VERY FEW LABELS PROVIDE AN INDICATION OF SWEETNESS, AND THOSE THAT DO TYPICALLY USE UNFAMILIAR TERMS.**

  Most premium wines are dry and their labels do not refer to sugar. However, some styles carry sweetness indicators. Deciding which metric to use is contentious since residual sugar is not always a reliable measure of perceptible sweetness. The chart on the next page is a rough sketch of sweetness terminology by corresponding residual sugar content.

WINE SWEETNESS TERMS

Dry Less than 10 grams/liter or 1%	**Brut** (France), **Sec** (France), **Trocken** (Germany), **Secco** (Italy)
Off-Dry/Medium Sweet 10–30 grams/liter or 1%–3%	**Demi-Sec/Doux** (France), **Halbtrocken** (Germany), **Abboccato/Amabile** (Italy)
Sweet/Dessert More than 30 grams/liter or 3%	**Moelleux/Liquoreux** (France), **Dolce** (Italy)

MARNIE'S CORNER

The word *dry* might just qualify as the most frustrating entry in the wine lexicon. Its meaning changes completely from its normal definition when applied to drinks such as wine or martinis. Normally, we understand *dry* to mean the opposite of *wet*, but when applied to beverages, *dry* means the opposite of sweet. A dry wine is one in which virtually all grape sugars have been converted to alcohol during fermentation. To further complicate matters, red wine contains *tannin*, a component that literally dries the mouth as though it's been blotted with a paper towel. But that is not what we mean when we describe a wine as *dry*.

So even though wines are clearly liquids, we call them *dry* when they're not sweet. And wines that physically dry the tongue are called *tannic*, not *dry*. Sheesh! No wonder people find wine lingo confusing!

WHITE VS. RED WINE:

DIFFERENCES RUN MORE THAN SKIN DEEP

GINA GALLO
Winemaker

THERE ARE ALL kinds of wines, but the best-known and most-popular categories are simply red and white. Not only are reds and whites made from different grapes, but two very different winemaking processes are required to produce them. Understanding how each process works can help you feel more comfortable choosing wine for any occasion.

• RED WINES GET THEIR COLOR FROM KEEPING SKINS WITH THE JUICE.

When looking at white, rosé, and red wines displayed on a store shelf, most of us picture the three colors of table grapes available in the supermarket: green, pale red, and dark purple. But it's not that simple. The flesh inside all those table grapes is translucent; only the skins have color. The same is true of wine grapes. Technically, white wine can be made from grapes of any color, but red wine can be made only from dark-skinned grapes. Whereas most white wines are made from green or yellow grapes, such as Chardonnay, some come from darker grapes, notably Pinot Grigio. Most Champagne-style sparkling wines are made with predominantly purple grapes, including Pinot Noir.

GINA GALLO is a third-generation winemaker and granddaughter of the famous California vintner Julio Gallo. She and Matt Gallo form a sister/brother team of winemaker and winegrower for Gallo Family Vineyards, which has been ranked among the world's most award-winning wineries since its first wines were released in 1993. She studied enology at the University of California at Davis and lives near the Sonoma winery.

- **RED WINES ARE "SKIN-DRIVEN" IN COLOR, FLAVOR, AND STYLE, WHEREAS WHITE WINES ARE "JUICE-DRIVEN."**

  The flavors in the skins of any fruit or vegetable differ from the flavors in the flesh. Red wines can be made only from dark-skinned grapes, and to acquire color they need to "soak" on their skins during the winemaking process. Grape skins have more flavor compounds, antioxidants, and vitamins than the juicy pulp and are more acidic than the flesh as well. Little wonder that red wines generally taste stronger and have more "pucker" than white wines—all these qualities come from fermenting on the skins. The flavors of white wines, which are made without skins, are generally simpler and milder. Without the skins, they showcase the qualities of fresh juice or peeled fruit.

- **RED WINES ARE FERMENTED IN CONTACT WITH GRAPE SKINS TO ACQUIRE COLOR AND FLAVOR, BEST DONE QUICKLY AT WARM TEMPERATURE.**

  In order to transfer the most color and flavor from the skins to the clear juice, red wines are made from whole fruit—skins, juice, pulp, seeds, and all. Heat helps enable this transfer, as when making a soup. Fermentation generates heat naturally, and the warmer the temperature, the faster the process. During the fermentation of red wines, we carefully monitor the temperature, usually keeping it between 65°F to 85°F (18°C to 30°C). We use just enough heat to help extract the color and flavor, but not so much that the process results in a "cooked" character. Fermenting whole grapes deepens and broadens the flavors of the fresh ingredients.

- **WHITE WINES ARE FERMENTED WITH THE JUICE ALONE TO RETAIN FRESHNESS AND ACIDITY, BEST DONE SLOWLY AT COLD TEMPERATURE.**

  The flavors in grape juice are subtler and more fragile than those in the robust skins. White winemaking is a balancing act as winemakers attempt to retain as much fresh fruit character as possible during fermentation. To achieve this balance, we first press the juice and separate it from the grape solids. Then we ferment the pure juice at colder temperatures—usually in the 45°F to 65°F (7°C to 18°C) range. If making red wine is akin to simmering tomato sauce for pasta, making white is like taking the same ingredients and making gazpacho.

- **PINK ROSÉ WINES BEGIN WITH BRIEF SKIN CONTACT, AS RED WINES DO, BUT ARE SOON PRESSED OFF AND FINISHED AS IF THEY WERE WHITE.**

  Rosés are the best of both worlds—boasting the refreshing tang of a white and a nice hint of satisfying red wine flavor. However, a downside to their "half and half" winemaking method is that the wines are delicious in youth but do not age as gracefully as their white or red counterparts. They taste so good, though, who wants to wait?

M ARNIE'S CORNER

Red wine and white wine are two different animals, each with different flavor possibilities based on the presence or absence of skins and their varied fermentation temperatures. "Skin-driven" red wines inevitably have bolder flavors than whites do, and they tend toward the fuller-bodied end of the spectrum. They also have mouth-drying tannins, imparted by the grape skins, that are simply not found in whites. After sipping red wine, the tannic astringency leaves a leathery feeling in the mouth. "Juice-driven" white wines, by contrast, almost always have a more understated flavor and are more refreshing. Whites can also do things red wines cannot, such as taste great with a hint of sweetness and deliver delicious flavor at low alcoholic strength.

GRAPE VARIETIES:
ONE GRAPE SPECIES, MANY VARIETALS

MICHAEL MONDAVI
Vintner

THE **GRAPES AVAILABLE** in supermarkets are great for eating. However, the low acidity, mild flavor, and thin skins that make them so table-friendly make them poorly suited as ingredients for wine. We need more intensely flavored fruit for winemaking, and we don't mind thick skins or seeds since these will be discarded. A grapevine species called *Vitis vinifera*, native to Europe, embodies the best qualities for vintners.

Vinifera may be a single species, but its grapes come in varied shapes, sizes, colors, and flavors. There are thousands of distinct varieties, just as with apples or melons. Wines made from these different varietals will taste noticeably different, which is one reason that grape categories are so often used to group wines by style and flavor. A small number of varieties have risen to the top in popularity and have the best track record for quality. Such names as Chardonnay and Shiraz are to wine grapes what Granny Smith and Red Delicious are to apples: varieties that lead the pack because most people like the way they taste.

Think about the world of citrus fruits. Lemons are very acidic but not very sweet. Limes are similar to lemons in tartness but different in flavor. Oranges are much sweeter and less sour, and grapefruits are bracingly tart

Scion of one of the world's most influential wine families, **MICHAEL MONDAVI** has more than 40 years of experience in the wine industry. After cofounding Robert Mondavi Winery with his father in 1966, he went on to manage the expanding business, eventually serving as president and CEO. In 2004 Michael teamed up with his wife, Isabel, and their children Rob and Dina to establish Folio Fine Wine Partners, an importer and producer of the most exciting quality wines from the world's premier and emerging wine regions, including Italy, Spain, Austria, New Zealand, Argentina, and California.

and pungently aromatic. The distinctions continue within each category: tangerines are less acidic than Valencia oranges, ruby grapefruits are sweeter than their white-fleshed cousins, and so on. Grape varieties differ from one another along similar lines. Riesling is a green grape, whereas Pinot Grigio looks red. Sauvignon Blanc is more acidic than Chardonnay. Cabernet Sauvignon is more intensely flavored than Merlot. (Wine producers have individual styles, of course, so these generalizations will not apply to every winemaker's production.)

• WHAT VARIES FROM ONE VARIETY TO THE NEXT?

In the vineyard, we can distinguish among grape varieties by sight. Leaves and clusters look different. Berry size and skin color vary widely, too. But, from a wine drinker's perspective, the important variables are those we notice in the wine, such as acidity, texture, and flavor profile. Most important, grape varieties yield wines that range in "body," or thickness in the mouth. Largely driven by alcohol content, body is what makes some wines seem lighter or heavier. In the same way that skim milk feels "lighter" than whole milk, wines made from Riesling are perceived as "lighter" than those made from Chardonnay grapes. Grape varieties differ in their overall acidity, or tartness, too; the Italian Sangiovese grape is notably sharper than, say, Zinfandel.

There is no right or wrong when it comes to such characteristics, just personal preferences. There's nothing wrong with preferring Merlot over Cabernet Sauvignon. And there is certainly no one "right grape" from the grower's perspective. Each variety has strengths and weaknesses, and we must carefully choose which to plant in each vineyard to get the best results. Some varieties prefer warmth, others like a cool breeze. Some perform best on stony hillsides, others in fertile valleys. In addition, there's a big difference in when each flowers in the spring and when it will be ready to harvest in the fall—as many as six weeks among some varietals in California.

• WHY LEARN ABOUT GRAPE VARIETIES?

Getting a feel for the flavor profile of the most popular fine-wine grape varieties can help you begin to untangle the overwhelming array of wines available. It's true that wines made from a particular grape will differ stylistically based on many other variables, including whether they come from a cool or a warm wine region or were made in a simple or ambitious fashion. But, in the big picture, there is enough family resemblance among them to serve as a useful guide in selecting wines.

More important, most wines are labeled by grape variety. Even those European wines that are still named the old-fashioned way—that is, by region—increasingly feature labels that state their main ingredient, even if it's in the fine print. Once you've found a few you like, you can continue to explore their various expressions from around the world. It's a fascinating form of vicarious travel. And remember: Many wines are blends of two or more varieties that taste great together.

BODY/STYLE	WHITE-WINE GRAPES	RED-WINE GRAPES
Light	Riesling Chenin Blanc	Pinot Noir Gamay
Medium	Sauvignon Blanc Pinot Grigio	Merlot Sangiovese
Full	Chardonnay Viognier	Cabernet Sauvignon Syrah / Shiraz

MARNIE'S CORNER

Wine is like a sauce that can be made from only one ingredient: grapes. Not surprisingly, even minor variations in that "raw material" will dramatically affect the final result. Grape variety is the first and most important variable for a wine novice to explore. Luckily, more and more wines are now clearly identified by grape variety on the label, whether overtly on the front or more surreptitiously on the back.

SUNSHINE AND WINE STYLE:
HOW CLIMATE AFFECTS BODY AND FLAVOR

————

LAURA MANIEC
Master Sommelier

———

I F ALL WINES from the same grape tasted alike, then varietal would be the only thing we need to know. But they don't. And as any winemaker will tell you, it's all about the weather. Take the example of Chardonnay. Warm, sunny Napa Valley is known for its bold, rich, and full-bodied Chardonnays, whereas those from the cooler, cloudier French region of Chablis are lighter, leaner, and subtler. Dozens of factors contribute to these distinctions, but the one that leaves the most dramatic imprint is climate, thanks to its impact on the ripening of the grapes.

Ripening is the final and most critical stage in the growth cycle of all fruits, for that is when they become edible. As fruits ripen, they grow sweeter, juicier, and more flavorful. Acids soften and color changes. Ripening requires a lot of energy and is fueled by the sun; therefore, the sunniest vineyards will always grow the sweetest fruit. Since sugar is converted into alcohol in the winemaking process, there is a direct connection between vineyard climate and wine style.

Think about growing tomatoes. Tomatoes start out green, hard, and sour. As the sun shines, the tomatoes turn bright red, becoming sweeter and less acidic. Sunlight ripens the fruit, producing lots of sugar and vivid "tomato-y" flavor and minimizing the perception of sourness. The same process

As director of wine and spirits for B. R. Guest Restaurants, **LAURA MANIEC** is responsible for selecting and purchasing all alcoholic beverages for 15 restaurants in cities across the country, including New York City, Chicago, and Las Vegas. She is also director of education for B. R. Guest Wine College, where she executes the training of 1,000 employees. In 2003, at age 22, Maniec was named Best New Sommelier of the Year by *Wine and Spirits Magazine*. She also teaches regularly at the French Culinary Institute and holds weekly blind-tasting groups with other New York City sommeliers.

occurs with grapes. Warm climates grow high-sugar grapes, and cool climates grow low-sugar grapes with more prominent acidity. Few concepts are as useful in making sense of the wine world as the impact of climate on flavor. Once you understand this idea, you'll be better equipped to make an educated guess about wine style before even pulling the cork.

- **TO MAKE THE BEST WINE, GRAPES SHOULD BE PERFECTLY RIPE.**
Winemakers waiting to harvest their vineyards test the ripeness of their grapes daily, waiting for the right time to pick. They need enough sugar and flavor to make good wine. But if ripening goes too far, fresh-tasting acids and aromatic complexity may be lost, just as peaches can go from delicious to bland if allowed to overripen.

- **FRUITS UNDERGO A DRAMATIC CHANGE AS THEY RIPEN, BECOMING SWEETER AND LESS SOUR, MORE FLAVORFUL AND LESS "GREEN."**
Green means "underripe" in any fruit. Unripe bananas, for example, look green and even impart a "green" taste. They're hard, starchy, not very sweet, and too acidic. The flavor we think of as "banana" doesn't fully develop until the banana turns yellow, softens, and sweetens. Grapes behave the same way; when underripe, they're sour and "green." As they ripen, they grow sweeter and sourness softens. As grape flavor strengthens, the underripe "green" flavor fades.

- **RIPENING IS POWERED BY SUNSHINE AND WARMTH. THE MORE SUN AND HEAT, THE FASTER THE GRAPES RIPEN.**
Think back to the example of the tomato. Those planted in the sunniest spots ripen quickly, whereas those in the shade lag behind. The same holds true for vineyards. Grapes grown in the coolest and cloudiest wine regions simply don't ripen as quickly or as completely as those from hotter and sunnier zones. They don't become as sweet, and they retain a noticeably higher acidity.

Warm and **Sunny**

Cool and **Cloudy**

High Sugar and Fruit Flavor
Low Acid and "Green" Flavor

Low Sugar and Fruit Flavor
High Acid and "Green" Flavor

Bold, Fruity,
Full-Bodied Wine

Subtle, Herbal,
Light-Bodied Wine

Since the ripening process is fueled by sunshine, climate dramatically affects grape flavor and, therefore, wine style.

- **WARM CLIMATES TYPICALLY YIELD HIGH-ALCOHOL, LOW-ACID WINES; COOL CLIMATES PRODUCE LOW-ALCOHOL, HIGH-ACID WINES.**

  Sun drives ripeness and sugar production during grape growing; sugar becomes alcohol during winemaking. What we perceive in wine as body is made possible by sunshine. The warmest regions will give us the strongest, heaviest wines, and the coolest will produce lighter wines with more tartness. Think back to the example of Napa Chardonnay compared to French Chablis. There are many differences between them, but the most obvious is that they lie on opposite ends of the ripeness spectrum.

	COOL CLIMATE/ LOW RIPENESS	WARM CLIMATE/ HIGH RIPENESS
Fruit Qualities	Less sweet/more acidic Less grapey/greener Low-intensity color/flavor	Sweeter/less acidic More grapey/less green High-intensity color/flavor
Wine Qualities	Lighter bodied/more tart Less fruity/more herbal Pale and subtle	Fuller bodied/less tart Fruitier/less herbal Vivid and bold
Wine Aromatics	White: apple, pear, citrus Red: cranberry, raspberry	White: peach, mango, fig Red: blackberry, cherry
Typical Styles	Sparkling, white, dessert	Red, rosé, fortified
Typical Regions	Northern France and Italy, Germany, Austria, New Zealand, Canada	California, Australia, Chile, Argentina, South Africa, Southern France, Spain

MARNIE'S CORNER

It's tempting to assume that more is always better when it comes to ripeness, but it's not quite that simple. Warm-climate wines can be impressive, monolithic even. But, when we push the ripeness envelope, there is danger of losing balance and complexity of aroma. Finesse is a specialty of cool-climate regions, whereas power is the hallmark of sunnier climes. In fact, some of the world's most highly regarded wines are decidedly cool-climate types, from Champagne to Barolo, French Burgundy to German Riesling. They are particularly prized as food partners, rather than as wines to drink alone.

TERROIR, OR THE "TASTE OF THE PLACE":

WHY REGION MATTERS IN WINE

———◆·•◆·•◆———

JEAN-LUC LE DÛ
Sommelier & Wine Retailer

A S A FRENCH sommelier, I am often asked about the concept of *terroir* (pronounced tair-*wahr*). Terroir is one of the organizing principles behind the fine-wine world. It is a logical concept, yet one that is surprisingly difficult to explain. Terroir sums up, in one word, all the myriad factors of geography and vineyard conditions that influence the flavor of the fruit grown in a particular place. Soil type and sun exposure, microclimate and microflora, all leave a flavor imprint on the grapes that can be perceived in the wine. Some aspects of terroir may be easily visible, such as the sunward-slope of Corton-Charlemagne. Others may be miles away from the vineyard, like the Vosges Mountains that shape the climate of Alsace.

It may sound strange to beginners, but fine wines can taste noticeably different from one vineyard to another, even when everything else is identical—grape variety and growing season, farming and winemaking. And the reverse is true as well. Two wines from the same vineyard will share a certain "family resemblance" even when made from two entirely different grape varieties. Science hasn't yet explained exactly how it happens, but it is simply true

JEAN-LUC LE DÛ ranks among New York City's leading wine professionals. As head sommelier of Daniel Boulud's Restaurant Daniel, he built one of the best wine programs in the United States, recognized with a Wine Spectator Grand Award. During his ten years with Boulud, Le Dû won the title of Sopexa's Best Sommelier Northeast America and the James Beard Foundation Award for Outstanding Wine Service. He now manages his independent venture, Le Dû's Wines, a tempera-ture-controlled wine store in the West Village that features artisanal winemakers and wines reflective of their terroir.

that we can taste the difference, like a fingerprint of a place. The more great wine you taste side by side, the more obvious the importance of terroir becomes.

- **TERROIR IS A WINE'S DISTINCTIVE REGIONAL CHARACTER, PART FLAVOR AND PART RESONANCE ON THE PALATE.**
Terroir refers to the influence of soil and landscape, climate and habitat, on growing grapes for wine. Expert tasters can recognize famous wines by smell and taste alone, by their distinctive *goût de terroir*, or, roughly, their "taste of the place." If we think in terms of music, terroir isn't the composer's melody or the musician's arrangement, but the unique acoustics of a particular performance venue. Every stage or studio has its own acoustics, but there is something different and compelling about the sound in the great ones, like Carnegie Hall or Electric Ladyland. If Jimi Hendrix had recorded somewhere else, his music would still have been great, but it would have sounded different.

- **TERROIR IS A FEATURE OF NATURE, BUT IT IS STRONGLY INFLUENCED BY PEOPLE.**
Just as great acoustics can be enhanced by design, the human hand can enhance terroir, as well. Natural farming that sustains the microbiological life of the vineyard environment can amplify the terroir character in wine. Interference in natural cycles, such as pesticides and irrigation, can mute that distinctive "voice" of the vineyard. Wines produced this way taste like foods that have been processed in a similar fashion—they may taste nice, but lack character.

- ***TERROIR* IS A FRENCH TERM THAT IS LIKE *EARTH* IN ENGLISH. IT MAY MEAN SIMPLY "SOIL" OR CONVEY A LARGER IDEA.**
For wine, it means roughly regional "typicity" or "sense of place." I must be very clear, though: Terroir is absolutely not exclusive to French wines. The idea may have originated in France, and it has great importance there—we speak about terroir for other products that have distinctive regionality too, such as cheeses, ducks, or olives—but every place on earth has its own terroir. No one region or product has a monopoly on this complex concept.

- **THE WORD *TERROIR* MAY APPLY TO THE WINE, THE LAND, OR BOTH.**

  The term most often describes a wine's distinctive characteristics, the "regional typicity" of flavor and style. Speaking of the terroir of traditional Chablis wines, we usually mean their distinctive minerality and finesse that can't be found in Chardonnays grown elsewhere. Sometimes, though, terroir can refer to the place itself, to a specific vineyard or district whose wines display such character. In this fashion, we might speak of "great terroirs," such as the Château Haut-Brion estate in Bordeaux, that produce highly individual wines of high quality. A wine's terroir is both the land on which the vines were grown and the unique characteristics of flavor and aroma that land imparts to the wine.

- **THE REGIONAL TYPICITY OF TERROIR LED WINES TO BE NAMED AND SOLD BY THEIR PLACE OF ORIGIN, HISTORICALLY, NOT BY THEIR GRAPE.**

  Because of the importance of terroir, in Europe wines are grouped under regional appellations, such as Burgundy, Bordeaux, Chianti, or Champagne. Centuries ago, the tastes of wines from every region differed greatly. For example, Burgundy wines from different villages, and even from vineyards higher or lower on the same slope, tasted noticeably different. Therefore, it was only natural that wines were named for their source, as with cheeses or teas, not for the names of the vines. Over time, some places showed consistent potential for making wine of great complexity. When combined with the right grape variety and carefully farmed to enhance their unique qualities, these vineyards could produce wines unlike any other. Wines from the finest terroirs earned name recognition, similar to luxury brands; villages like Margaux and vineyards like Le Montrachet commanded a premium and came to be known for specific styles. The European system of appellations, or regulated regional wine names, is rooted in this concept: that wine from every place will taste different, and those from the same source will share a certain regional typicity, or *goût de terroir*.

MARNIE'S CORNER

We are all products of our environments, of our countries and cultures, neighborhoods and schools. Our upbringing reflects the values of our parents and our communities. Wines have a similar identity, a reflection of their origin and the values of their growers. Among mass-produced wines, this character can be obscured. But the finest wines are often those true to their terroir; those that sing out their individuality in an unmistakable way.

UNDERSTANDING OAK:

THE ROLE OF BARRELS IN WINEMAKING

◆·◆·◆·◆

TOM STEVENSON
Wine Author

J UST AS A chef may use spices to enhance the flavor of a dish, winemakers use oak to adjust the taste and texture of their wines. Oak can add desirable aromatic qualities, but as with all condiments, it should be used sparingly. Barrels also soften a wine, just as slow-cooking tenderizes a tough cut of meat. Oak treatment brings forward a wine's development, making it easier and more pleasurable to drink when it is still relatively young. Oaked wines are neither superior nor inferior, however, for barrel treatment is more flattering to some wine styles than others.

Other woods have been used for wine barrels, but they are either high in undesirable resins and oils, such as chestnut, or too porous to be practical, like pine. Oak is low in porosity, making it dense enough to contain liquids, yet it can be easily bent into rounded shapes. It also has an acceptable tannin content and mild aromatic compounds that harmonize intrinsically with wine. More than 99.9 percent of wine barrels are made of oak, as are those used for whiskies and brandies.

Oak barrels were first used by the Romans for the practical purpose of transporting wine. These convenient vessels proved able to boost wine's flavor and texture.

TOM STEVENSON is the author of *The New Sotheby's Wine Encyclopedia*, widely considered to be the standard industry reference for the wine trade. He is also the world's foremost authority on the wines of Champagne. He has written prolifically about wine for more than 30 years, producing 23 critically acclaimed books and receiving 30 awards for wine writing. An occasional contributor to *Decanter* magazine and columnist for *The World of Fine Wine* and the online magazine "Wine-pages," he is founding editor of DK's ground-breaking *Wine Report* books, an annual series detailing the state of the wine world.

European winemakers gradually learned to ferment and store wines in barrels, with sizes varying by region. It was only in modern times, when the growing scale of winemaking demanded the use of much larger stainless-steel tanks for fermentation, that we realized, through constant comparison, precisely what fermentation and aging in oak bring to a wine.

- **OAK IS NOT INERT. BARRELS CAN IMPART VARIOUS AROMATIC QUALITIES TO WINE, MOST NOTABLY A DISTINCTIVE, SWEET, AND CREAMY NUANCE.**
  Typical oak aromas include vanilla (from vanillin, which is found both in oak and in vanilla pods) and coconut (usually American oak species). Aromas of toast, coffee, cloves, smoke, cedar, and tobacco are usually derived from the barrel's degree of "toast," the charring by flame that helps bend the staves. This process directly influences a wine's flavor.

- **WOOD IS POROUS, SO BARRELS ARE NOT AIRTIGHT; WINE STORED IN BARRELS UNDERGOES BOTH SLOW OXIDATION AND SLOW EVAPORATION.**
  Wood's porosity is especially significant for red wines. It is the microscopic ingress of oxygen that softens a wine stored in oak. And of course this transfer is a two-way street. Just as air can seep into barrels, so too can gases leak out. Water and alcohol evaporate slowly through the wood, concentrating flavor—a factor that should not be underestimated.

- **RED WINES CAN HANDLE MORE OAK TREATMENT THAN WHITES, AND SOME MAY REQUIRE IT. MANY WHITES NEED NO OAK AT ALL.**
  Barrel maturation is almost essential for fine red wines, mellowing those made from intense grapes such as Cabernet Sauvignon and Shiraz. Oak use is more of a stylistic choice when making white wine; it is better suited to enhancing neutral grapes like Chardonnay than aromatic varieties such as Riesling.

- **OAK CHARACTERISTICS DO NOT ALWAYS COME FROM BARRELS.**
Since oak aromas are popular, many wines mass produced in stainless steel are "flavored" with oak. A long soak with oak chips, shavings, or staves can impart a toasty woody scent without the expense or effort of racking wine in and out of barrels. Such wine, however, will not benefit from oak's softening properties unless the steel tanks are fitted with micro-oxygenation technology, which slowly releases microscopic bubbles of oxygen into the wine.

- **WHEN SELECTING BARRELS, WINEMAKERS CONSIDER VARIOUS FACTORS.**
Barrels are remarkably diverse, so winemakers face many choices on the road to achieving their desired results. The most important variables are:

1. **SIZE.** The smaller the barrel, the greater the ratio of wood surface to wine, thus the more aromatic compounds a wine will extract from the oak.
2. **AGE.** When an oak barrel is first used, it imparts the most aromatic compounds to a wine. Like resteeping a tea bag, however, this flavor will fade with each use. The older the oak, the less aromatic influence it will have.
3. **OAK SPECIES.** American white oaks are fast growing and wide grained, whereas European brown oaks grow more slowly and with tighter grain. Industry consensus is that American barrels tend to add more obvious coconut-y aromas, and French barrels produce subtler aromas and add more tannins.
4. **BARREL-MAKING, OR COOPERAGE.** Cooperage techniques vary by region and by barrel maker, with the quality-oriented traditions originating in France. Some Europhile snobs say that American oak is big, brash, and vulgar. However, much of the difference is caused more by the humans involved than by the trees. American oak may be coarser grained, but its lack of refinement also results from rupturing the grain. To expedite production and control costs, American oak is sawed and kiln dried, which concentrates the vanillin and lactones. French oak is split along the grain and seasoned outdoors to leach excessive aroma compounds

and harsh tannins. If French oak were treated the American way, it would taste just as big, brash, and vulgar.

5. **BARREL TOAST.** In barrel-making, an open flame is used to heat barrel staves before they are rounded into shape. The resulting degree of charring on the barrel interior is known as "toast," and it varies from light to heavy. Aromatic properties range from the natural wood character of light toast to the caramelized qualities of medium toast. Heavy toast, with its charred-smoke flavor, is more commonly used for whiskey.

M ARNIE'S CORNER

Since wine is made 100 percent from grapes, the flavor of oak is generally the only foreign "seasoning" used in winemaking. But many wine lovers have difficulty distinguishing oak smells from grape or wine smells. The scents associated with oak are distinctive and have much in common with those found in brown spirits such as whiskey and brandy. The aroma of Cognac is dominated by the toasty vanilla aroma of French oak, and Bourbon and California brandy display a more distinctive, coconut-y, American oak character.

OLD WORLD/NEW WORLD:

DIFFERENCES IN PHILOSOPHY AND FLAVOR

———◆·◆·◆———

RANDALL GRAHM
Winemaker

I T MAY SOUND dated to speak of *Old World* and *New World*, but such terms do describe a wine concept of up-to-the-minute relevance. They are particularly useful when explaining the differences in both wine styles among producers and wine tastes among consumers. The winemaking style of classic Old World regions, including France and Italy, is rooted in centuries of tradition and emphasizes distinctiveness, or typicity. *Terroir* is the term used to describe the individuality of a given site for grapes, its flavor fingerprint independent of the stylistic inputs of the winemaker. The Old World is, or at least once was, more focused on celebrating the special characteristics inherent in each vineyard, whether the soil types that impart unique flavor characteristics or the distinctive differences among vintages. New World regions such as the United States and Chile, by contrast, are pioneering an approach that relies more on technological innovation and stylized winemaking formulas to achieve commercial acceptance. The newcomers are most comfortable in the position of control, from irrigation of the vineyards to cultured strains of yeast. This approach leaves little to chance, trusting in better living through wine chemistry.

RANDALL GRAHM is the founder and fearless leader of Bonny Doon Vineyard and one of California's most eccentric and influential vintners. Like Columbus seeking a trade route to Asia, Grahm set sail in 1979 for the Great American Pinot Noir, foundered on the shoals of astringency and finesselessness, and ended up running aground in the utterly unexpected New World of Rhône and Italian grape varieties. A citizen of the world, he is perhaps best known as a champion of the strange and the heterodox, of the ugly duckling grape varietals whose very existence is threatened by the dominant Cabo- and Chardo-centric paradigms.

"Every year is a vintage year" is the mantra, and indeed the consistency of New World wines is a great part of their success.

The concept of an Old World/New World style continuum is, of course, a sweeping generalization to which many exceptions exist. But the metaphor is useful in helping to explain a pattern of tangible "taste-able" differences. Broadly speaking, Old World wines tend to be less alcoholic and more acidic, more "mineral" and less "fruit" driven than their New World counterparts. The old-fashioned style prides itself on complexity and balance, factors that enhance compatibility with food. The new-fangled style shoots instead for power and flavor density, hoping to earn top scores from an attention deficit-afflicted media through seductive first impressions, which are often cued by the presence of new oak.

This Old World/New World concept sounds like an either/or question of geography alone, but that view is overly simplistic. The real differences are more about human nature than Mother Nature, and the results are far from black and white. Our sensibilities and priorities—economical, cultural, agricultural—shape our actions. Old World and New World are mindsets: They are different perspectives on what we're trying to achieve when we make wine.

- **ONCE UPON A TIME, ALL WINE WAS EUROPEAN (OR RATHER EURASIAN), AND UNTIL RECENTLY THE BEST WINES WERE INDISPUTABLY SO.**
A little history is essential to understanding this strange bipolar wine-iverse that we inhabit. Great wines from such places as California and Australia are a recent phenomenon. Wine grapes were first domesticated thousands of years ago in the Caucasus and then spread, first west toward the balmy Mediterranean and then north into cooler western Europe. Fine wine traditions were pioneered by medieval French monastic orders. By sacrificing quantity for quality, and after centuries of careful observation and iteration, monks grew better fruit and crafted distinctive wines worthy of reverence. They inspired other regions to try producing better wine too, with each region working with their own indigenous grape varieties. For example, while the Burgundy region grew Chardonnay and Pinot Noir, the Bordeaux area was home to Cabernet Sauvignon and Merlot.

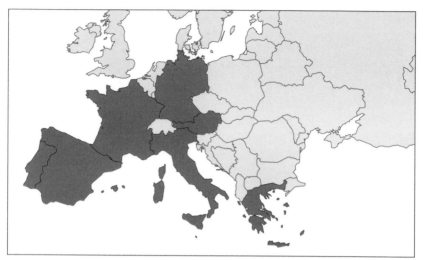

Old World. *France, Italy, Germany, Spain, Austria, Portugal, Greece*

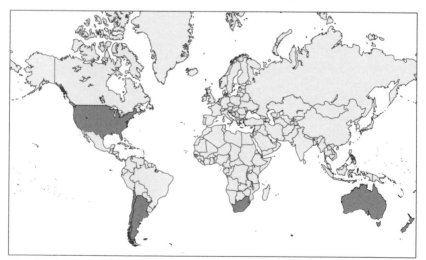

New World. *United States, Australia, Chile, New Zealand, South Africa, Argentina*

- **WHEN EUROPEAN COLONISTS LAID CLAIM TO THE SO-CALLED NEW WORLD, OLD WORLD GRAPES AND WINEMAKING KNOW-HOW CAME ALONG FOR THE RIDE.**

  Europeans planted their crops, including grapevines, throughout the Americas and the Southern Hemisphere. At first the mainstay was highly productive workhorse grapes, such as Zinfandel, Mataro (aka Mourvedre), and Shiraz (in Antipodia), but eventually pioneering vintners desirous of producing better wines began planting pedigreed French vines. However, because the grapes were not always grown in the most appropriate areas, initial efforts with grapes like Chardonnay and Merlot were hardly recognizable as familial relations to their Old World counterparts. In the late twentieth century, the dominance of "technical" wines has often blurred the expressiveness of place that we may still find in Old World wines.

- **OLD WORLD WINE TRADITIONS HAD EVOLVED OVER CENTURIES TOWARD REGIONAL DISTINCTIVENESS, FOOD FRIENDLINESS, AND AGING POTENTIAL.**

  In Europe, the finest wines always came from challenging environments, places where the combination of cool climate and poor soil forced vines to struggle, to yield smaller amounts of more flavorful fruit. Winemaking techniques developed by trial and error, without electricity or microscopes, with the goal of making long-lived wines that resisted the relentless march of oxidation and decline. Regional styles naturally flattered local cuisine, since performance was judged at the table. Most of all, a wine's individuality was its badge of honor. The finest wines had their own unique character, just as works of art do. With the advent of the twentieth century, Europe began regulating its wine industry around regional typicity, naming each wine by its unique source and generally encouraging vintners to make less wine in order to improve its quality and distinctiveness.

	OLD WORLD	NEW WORLD
Countries	France, Italy, Germany, Spain, Austria, Portugal, Greece	United States, Australia, Chile, New Zealand, South Africa, Argentina
Wines Tend to Be	Lower in alcohol Lighter in body Very dry Higher in acidity More subtle in aromas More "earthy" or "herbal," or "mineral" Capable of longer aging in bottle More resistant to oxidation after opening	Higher in alcohol Fuller in body Not as dry Lower in acidity Bolder in aromas More "fruity" or "jammy" Designed for earlier enjoyment

- **SUCCESS IN NEW WORLD WINE CULTURE IS DEFINED BY COMMERCIAL APPEAL, FAVORABLE FIRST IMPRESSIONS, AND INSTANT GRATIFICATION.**

  New World vineyards were most often sited in regions that were much warmer and drier than Europe's fine wine zones, where poor weather poses an annual risk. From California to Australia, Chile to South Africa, irrigation in near-desert conditions allowed lush vines to grow virtually risk free. With ample sunshine and added water, grapes ripen quickly, growing sweeter, juicier, and more intensely fruity. Challenging the European ideal of complexity in the 1970s, New World wines staked a claim to a riper, more fruit-driven style. Advanced technology and a near-obsessive need to control microbial life in wines led to squeaky-clean wines that banished complex scents and tasted primarily of jammy fruit. Without a historical context, wines were judged in blind tastings, leading to excessive emphasis on power over balance, ripeness over complexity, prettiness over beauty. Like Hollywood remakes of classic European films, New World wines were attention-getting blockbusters, but lacked finesse.

- **OLD WORLD AND NEW WORLD WERE ONCE CLEAR-CUT EXTREMES BUT ARE NOW BETTER UNDERSTOOD AS TWO ENDS OF A WINE-STYLE SPECTRUM.**

Over the last few decades, the global expansion of fine wine has become big business, and the influence of commercialism is felt everywhere. To appeal to markets used to the juicy New World style, many European producers now tailor their wines to suit fruitier tastes and to impress powerful wine critics in particular. Although some of these wines are of high quality, only the most steadfast have resisted the inevitable lurch toward sameness that occurs when focus groups set winemaking priorities. But it's also true that a growing number of vintners in the Americas and the Southern Hemisphere are recognizing the palate fatigue and boredom induced by a parade of top-heavy, look-alike wines. Some are simply making brighter wines better suited to the table, and others are reviving old traditions of grape growing and winemaking. It's rare to find wines that completely transcend their region's heritage, though many are creeping toward the middle ground. Country of origin was once enough to predict how a wine would taste. Now it's less certain, but the old patterns remain a useful guide.

MARNIE'S CORNER

Few concepts are more useful in guesstimating wine style than the Old World/New World concept. Some people will always prefer one over the other, and others may switch sides, depending on the occasion or the meal. In general, the New World style is more approachable, whereas the Old World style can be more of an acquired taste. There are strong opinions and snobbery on both sides, but neither is right or wrong. Tastes in wine are as personal as tastes in music, fashion, or art.

CHAPTER
TWO

Wine Tasting

J UST AS YOU DON'T NEED AN ART-APPRECIATION CLASS TO APPRECIATE ART, YOU DON'T NEED A WINE-TASTING CLASS TO ENJOY TASTING WINE. CRACK OPEN THAT BOTTLE AND have a glass. But if your curiosity extends beyond the everyday, it's well worth examining the act of tasting, learning what to do and what to look for. A simple change in how you sip can intensify the wine experience, and discovering how your senses operate will boost your confidence. A mental checklist of basic characteristics will allow you to compare each new wine to others you've tried. Learning the definitions of basic tasting terms can help dramatically as well, especially when it comes to interpreting label language or wine reviews.

I always recommend that newcomers focus first on wine tasting before worrying about regions or grapes. For most, data-heavy wine study is impractical. However, training ourselves to be better tasters is easy and fun, and any day can be an opportunity to practice our skills. Besides, learning wine-tasting lingo gives us tools we'll need in case we do decide to take the next step, committing detailed wine information to memory.

You'll hear people say that wine tasting is subjective, and this is certainly true of preferences, which vary as widely as tastes in music or fashion. Individuals often describe smells in different terms, and sensitivity to taste or smell varies from one person to the next. But wine tasting is not entirely nebulous. There are objective characteristics that professionals use to categorize wine styles: taste qualities such as sweetness, tactile qualities like body, and aromatic qualities including the scent of new oak. Such features are the wine "signposts" that anyone can learn to recognize.

HOW TO TASTE WINE LIKE A PRO

RICHARD BETTS

Master Sommelier & Winemaker

TASTING WINE COMES naturally. When we encounter something so delicious, we savor the experience, much as we might a piece of music or beautiful painting. For most wine drinkers, such enjoyment is more than enough. But it's true that enjoyment unexamined doesn't help us learn. The next day we'll remember only that we liked the wine, but not why. To become a better taster, the first step is to develop a consistent approach.

Because our senses fluctuate as widely as our emotions, wine will taste different under varied circumstances; for example, we enjoy a wine more if we're on vacation than if we have to work the next day. Humans are such variable beings that we need a methodology to clearly observe wines and compare them in the same light. Approaching every wine consistently—assessing the same characteristics—allows us to mentally file it within a larger context. Our mental checklist prompts us to look for, and therefore remember, distinctive qualities.

Professionals evaluate wine one sense at a time. We begin with how a wine looks in the glass before moving on to how it smells. From there we take a sip, which allows us to note both how it tastes and how it feels in the mouth. Lastly, we observe how wine components resonate after swallowing.

RICHARD BETTS is a master sommelier, one of only a handful to pass the rigorous examination on the first attempt. During his tenure as wine director for Aspen's premier restaurant Montagna at The Little Nell, Betts built one of the country's most ambitious wine programs. In 2008 he passed on the reins at Montagna to set out on the next phase of his career: becoming a vintner and winemaker, with the help of partner Dennis Scholl. Together they launched Betts and Scholl, making wines from around the world in partnership with some of the globe's top growers.

Some important wine attributes make themselves most apparent in the "finish," literally the wine's aftertaste. That is also where we can relax and enjoy the ride.

1. START WITH YOUR EYES. LOOK AT THE WINE AGAINST A WHITE BACKGROUND.

Tilt the glass away from yourself and look closely at the wine's color. White wines range from nearly clear to deep gold. Both age and barrels darken whites over time by slow oxidation, in the same way that sliced apples brown when exposed to air. Red wines oxidize too, moving from pink-purple in youth to rust-brown in maturity. Unlike whites, reds grow paler with age as suspended pigment particles settle as sediment. Because thick-skinned grapes impart more color, Shiraz will always look darker than Pinot Noir, for example. But color has no taste, so although its depth may look impressive, that doesn't mean the flavor is improved. Another visible style factor is wine's viscosity, which is observable after we swirl the glass. Both alcohol and sugar make wine seem thick in texture. The slower the beads of wine form and stream down the glass, the richer and fuller bodied the wine will feel in the mouth.

2. SWIRL THE WINE AND TAKE A SNIFF. CLOSE YOUR EYES. WHAT DO YOU SMELL?

Smell is a preview of a wine's flavor, and the olfactory dimension is the most important part of tasting, before, during, and after each sip. Once critical for survival, our powerful sense of smell has been increasingly marginalized in modern life. Scents trigger a lifetime's worth of vivid memories—go with the smells wherever they take you. Allow yourself to form free associations and describe them to yourself. With practice, professionals learn to recognize and classify wine scents into three main groups: fruit, earth, and wood smells. The words you choose do not matter; highly personal associations work just as well as industry jargon. Naming the smell is what helps recall it later, whether it's "lemon," "French oak," or "Santa Fe on a rainy day."

3. TAKE A SIP AND SWISH IT AROUND FOR A COUPLE SECONDS TO COAT THE PALATE.

Professionals tasting many wines will spit to keep their heads clear. But even if you swallow, you must allow the wine to hit every surface of your mouth, in a similar way to using mouthwash. When the wine hits the tip of the tongue, notice if it is dry or imparts a hint of sweetness. Inhale after swallowing and reassess the aromas as they become flavors. What began as general impressions of fruit, wood, and earth may coalesce into specifics, such as blueberry or cherry, vanilla or caramel, mushrooms or wet gravel. Acidity makes itself known as a zing along the sides of the tongue that causes your mouth to water. By contrast, tannin has no taste but manifests itself as a tactile sensation after swallowing, as though the tongue were being dried with a towel. When in the mouth, alcohol feels thicker than water, giving a textural sensation of body. Light-bodied wines feel sheer, like water, and full-bodied wines feel richer, like a milkshake.

4. TAKE A MINUTE TO CONTEMPLATE THE WINE, NOTING ITS FINISH.

Great wines can reverberate on the palate for minutes after they've been swallowed—similar to the elongated note of a tuning fork—whereas poorly made wines often fall with a thud. Wine professionals judge quality by observing the interplay of lingering flavors, taste, and tactile sensations. Is the wine balanced or askew? How much "length" is in the finish? Only careful farming and winemaking can produce this resonance, and it is completely independent of color or power scale. A long and harmonious finish distinguishes fine wine, regardless of whether it is as delicate as Champagne or as dense as Amarone.

Figure A. *Tilt the glass away from yourself and look at the wine's color.*

Figure B. *Swirl the wine to release its aromas, then observe how it coats the glass.*

Figure C. *Sniff the wine to preview its flavor. Describing the scents helps boost memory.*

Figure D. *Take a sip. Swish the wine around in your mouth to amplify taste, smell, and tactile sensations.*

MARNIE'S CORNER

Many people have difficulty tasting the differences among wines, but a simple change in the way you sip can fix that problem. Because wine is strongly flavored and alcoholic, we tend to take teeny tiny sips, allowing the wine to trickle down the center of the tongue to the throat. But to really notice a wine's distinctive characteristics, we need as much sensory information as possible. Professionals allow the wine to hit every taste bud and coat every surface of the mouth. We hold the wine in the mouth long enough to warm it slightly—which volatilizes aroma compounds—and inhale after swallowing to deliver those flavorful vapors up the back of the nose. Think of tasting wine as using mouthwash, and before you know it you'll be making funny faces and gurgling noises like a pro. You'll be so amazed at how this method amplifies sensations that you'll be tempted to do the same with other beverages, such as coffee and juices.

HOW TO FIND WORDS FOR WINE'S ELUSIVE AROMAS

ANN NOBLE
Wine Educator

W E MAY CALL it wine "tasting," but most of what we think of as flavor is actually perceived by our sense of smell. We tend to define aroma as something we sniff with the nose, and taste as something perceived with the tongue. But biologically speaking, taste buds are limited in the messages they can transmit. Alone, they can detect the presence of only a handful of characteristics on contact: sweet, sour, salty, bitter, and umami (the "yum" taste of glutamates). Aroma is responsible for delivering much of what we describe as "taste," that is, the complex flavors of food and wine.

It's natural for the brain to locate flavor as being present in the mouth, of course, since the sensation occurs when we sip a beverage or bite into food. And for everyday wine drinking, it hardly matters which sensory organ perceives what. The olfactory sensations responsible for wine flavor blend seamlessly with taste and tactile sensations to form our experience of wine as a whole.

Understanding how taste and smell work together is not truly required for enjoying wine. But if we want to communicate about wine style and flavor—to decipher wine reviews or read labels—then knowing the difference between taste and scent is extremely useful. Identifying

DR. ANN C. NOBLE, professor emerita of enology at the University of California at Davis, is best known for the creation of the Wine Aroma Wheel, a popular tool for developing descriptive wine vocabulary. Professor Noble taught courses and conducted research in sensory evaluation of wine for the university's Department of Viticulture and Enology. She is now consulting, teaching short courses, and presenting seminars on wine sensory evaluation in the United States and abroad. She also serves as a wine judge in national and international wine shows. The Wine Aroma Wheel is available online in many languages.

which pathway wine's various messages take on their way to the brain helps us classify them and zero in on specific characteristics. Communicating about flavor and scent is a real challenge since there are no obvious reference points, such as red or blue, hot or cold, that we can use to orient ourselves. Yet for wine enthusiasts and professionals, building a descriptive vocabulary is well worth the effort.

- **WHAT WE THINK OF AS "FLAVOR" ISN'T MOSTLY TASTE, IT'S MOSTLY SMELL.**

  Inhaling through the nose brings volatile aroma compounds such as esters into the nasal cavity. There, they encounter the olfactory region and are detected as scents. When we sip wine or take a bite of food, a similar phenomenon happens, but from a different direction. The volatile compounds still travel to the olfactory center, but through the "back door," up the back of your nose where it meets your throat. In fact, scents are often more vivid when tasted than when sniffed, as they are amplified by proximity and the warming action of body heat.

- **AROMAS ARE HARDER FOR MOST OF US TO DESCRIBE THAN ARE TASTES AND TEXTURES.**

  Sensations perceived with the taste buds are fairly easy to distinguish for most tasters: sweet or dry, for example. Tactile sensations are straightforward, too: warm or cold, light or heavy (a wine's "body"). Describing aromas is more challenging. There are no "primary scents" to correspond with the "primary colors" that help us describe the spectrum. Instead, we have hundreds of volatile compounds that interact in a way we don't fully understand. Some compounds have a distinctive aroma, such as the smell of bell peppers so often found in Cabernet Sauvignon and Merlot wines. Other aromas are caused by multiple compounds and can be harder to pin down. For example, vanilla, cinnamon, and wintergreen perceived together form what most people think of as another distinct smell: bubblegum.

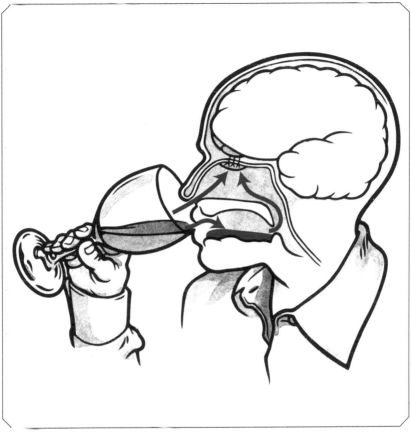

Wine's most distinctive characteristics are olfactory, perceived as "scent" when we sniff wine but also as "flavor" when we take a sip.

- **WORDS FOR SCENTS HELP US RECALL WINE EXPERIENCES.**
Without words to describe a wine, we remember only that we liked or disliked it. By attaching a few words to it, we give ourselves a fighting chance to remember the flavor in detail.

- **LEARNING AROMA WORDS IS EASY; JUST FOLLOW YOUR NOSE.**
Very few people are naturally oriented to their sense of smell, but all it takes is conscious effort. Building a descriptive aroma lexicon simply requires some smell exploration. Search out scents and practice connecting them to words. Most wine scents are foodlike, so take an aroma tour of the produce aisle, spice rack, or tea shop. While smelling the ingredient, repeat the name to yourself or write it down to help embed the memory. Check out other scents, anything from soaps and flowers to types of lumber. Once you start sniffing around, you'll find all sorts of smells you never consciously noticed before.

MARNIE'S CORNER

One reason that we find wine so mystifying at first is that scent plays such a strong role in our perception of it. Our sense of smell has been marginalized as we've grown more "civilized." Sights and sounds are now the dominant means by which we evaluate our world. But there's a primeval quality about aroma that makes it seductive. Smell has been shown to trigger vivid memories, particularly those with an emotional component. Wine is unusually diverse in the aromas and scents it captures. Next time you're savoring a terrific wine, take a nice deep sniff and ask yourself, "What does this smell remind me of?" You might just find yourself transported to another place and time.

HOW TO DETERMINE
WHETHER A WINE IS DRY

JEAN TRIMBACH
Vintner

D RY IS A peculiar term to apply to a drink. It cannot be taken literally since wine is so clearly wet. When used to describe beverages, *dry* simply means the opposite of sweet. Interestingly, this same metaphor is found in many languages: *sec* in French, *trocken* in German, *secco* in Italian, and so on. In each language, the everyday word for "not wet" is used to describe wines that are not sweet.

Most wines are dry because winemaking naturally converts the sugar in grapes to alcohol. When fermentation runs its course, wine reaches its full alcoholic strength and sugar is depleted. Dry wines are also naturally stable, since small amounts of residual sugar leave wine susceptible to spoilage. For centuries, dry has been the norm for wine, especially for fine wines. Dry wines are refreshing and make exceptionally versatile food partners. Modern wine drinkers prefer dry wines in general, as we can observe in the market. If sweet wine was everyone's preference, more would be made that way.

Yet there is no question that there is a place for wines with sweetness too. Some foods call for sweet wines, and dry wines can be an acquired taste. Wine novices tend to favor wines with a little pleasing sweetness, those reminiscent of fruit juice. This is one reason most inexpensive bulk wines

JEAN TRIMBACH is a twelfth-generation French vintner whose family name is synonymous with fine Alsace wine. Renowned worldwide for its quality, Maison Trimbach is the Alsace region's highest-profile wine producer. Trimbach manages the business and export markets, and his brother Pierre oversees the vineyards and winery. Before entering the family business, Jean spent a year studying the wine industry, from marketing in New York to winemaking in Napa Valley to operations in Bordeaux. Since 1985 he has traveled extensively, representing Trimbach wines and acting as unofficial ambassador for the Alsace region.

aren't fully dry. (Another reason is that sugar can mask wine defects nicely.) Biologically, sugar is an energy source that we are hard-wired to appreciate. Most of the famous styles of sweet wine—from lightly sweet Vouvray to sticky-sweet Sauternes—were first made by mistake. We now replicate these "happy accidents" deliberately.

Perhaps no other sensory component of wine causes so much misunderstanding. And unfortunately there is also disagreement in the industry about how to convey sweetness information on labels. Here are some helpful insights into dryness and sweetness in wine.

- **SWEETNESS IS PERCEIVED WITH THE TASTE BUDS, AND MOST VIVIDLY NEAR THE TIP OF THE TONGUE.**
  The presence or absence of sugar can be detected only by tasting wine, not by sight or smell, though the color of dessert wines may often hint at their depth of sweetness. Like other taste bud sensations, we notice sweetness immediately on contact with the tongue. Individuals can be more or less sensitive to sweetness, but most people can definitively identify the presence of sugar in wine when it reaches 10 to 15 grams per liter.

- **WINES WITH NO DETECTABLE SWEETNESS ARE KNOWN AS "DRY," AND THOSE WITH FAINT SWEETNESS ARE CALLED "OFF-DRY." ONLY EXTREME SWEETNESS IS CALLED "SWEET."**
  The language of sweetness and dryness is not exactly intuitive. Think of it as a linear scale, from bone-dry to dry to off-dry to sweet. Only when a wine approaches the sugary sweetness of grape juice or candy do we describe it as sweet; these types are known as dessert wines. The term *off-dry* simply means "not completely dry." (Picture the faint sweetness of one spoon of sugar in tea.) "Bone-dry" is an imaginative way to describe wines that are extremely dry.

- **PERCEIVED DRYNESS OR SWEETNESS DOES NOT ALWAYS CORRELATE WITH MEASUREMENTS OF SUGAR CONTENT.**

  If it were that simple, wines could note sugar content on their labels, as they do for alcohol, as an indicator of style. But some types of sugars seem sweeter than others, and other components in the wine can either mask or amplify the perceived sweetness. Elevated acidity and carbonation can block sweetness, whereas elevated alcohol can mimic a sweet taste. For example, "brut" Champagne, which contains as much as 15 grams of sugar per liter, may taste completely dry, but a California Chardonnay with less than half the residual sugar may taste palpably sweeter.

- **SINCE THE DEGREE OF SWEETNESS IS CONTROLLED BY THE WINEMAKER, ANY GRAPE CAN BE MADE INTO EITHER A SWEET OR A DRY STYLE.**

  Our modern mastery of winemaking allows us to achieve whatever result is desired, from fully sweet to fully dry and anywhere in between. It is true that we associate sweetness with wines from certain regions and grapes, but that is the result of tradition, not an inherent quality of the fruit. For example, Riesling wines are widely assumed to be sweet, but some are and others are not. Although German and American Rieslings usually retain some sweetness, those made in Alsace are traditionally very dry, as are many from Australia and Austria. In each of these zones, winemakers may choose whether to honor tradition or to step outside its limits.

- **PERCEIVED SWEETNESS WILL CHANGE OVER TIME; AS WINES AGE, THEY WILL ALWAYS TASTE DRIER, NEVER SWEETER.**

  Although sugar content remains technically constant, wines seem less sweet on the palate after long-term aging. In youth, wines display the most sweetness they will ever have. If a fine wine seems overly sweet on release, it simply requires some patience. Returning to the bottle years later, it will always taste a little drier. This is particularly noticeable in great dessert wines that have aged for decades. Of course, well-made dry wines age well, too.

MARNIE'S CORNER

Sweetness is a major wine style factor, and it ranks among the first characteristics we learn to recognize. Most wine drinkers have a clear preference for either drier or sweeter wines, and they are frustrated that wines are rarely marked clearly. In fact, terms like *dry* may appear on the labels of wines that are anything but. If salsa can be labeled mild, medium, and hot, why not label wines *dry*, *off-dry*, and *sweet*? This proposition may sound sensible, but vintners resist referring to sweetness on labels unless doing so is established regional tradition. One problem is that there is little agreement on where to draw the line. Not only do individuals perceive sweetness differently, but cultures do as well. Wines considered dry in the United States may seem sugary to Italians. Food context is a major factor; sugar in food makes wine taste dramatically drier, and American food is sweeter than the cuisine of most countries. However, widespread among consumers is the erroneous association of sweetness with low quality. That perception is entirely inaccurate; there are, of course, world-class off-dry and sweet wines. But since cheap wines are often sugary and premium wines are often dry, it is sad but true that advertising sweetness can have a negative impact on perceived quality.

HOW TO DETECT AND MAKE SENSE OF ACIDITY IN WINE

MICHAEL WEISS
Wine Educator

A CIDITY IS A defining trait of wine. The acids found in wine give it a bracing tartness when it hits the tongue, similar to the sensations found in tasting Granny Smith apples or grapefruit. Acidity is a crucial factor in wine's ability to age gracefully and is largely responsible for its ability to pair so well with food. It creates a resonance on the palate that extends the aftertaste of any food or wine in an appetizing way, making us hungrier and thirstier with every sip.

Acids are organic compounds that impart a sour taste to foods and beverages. Wines are high in acidity—far more so than beer or spirits—because fresh fruit is also naturally high in acids. Grapes are packed with tartaric acid, along with some malic acid and citric acid, too. More acids can be generated during the winemaking process—some good, such as lactic acid, and some bad, including acetic acid. Technically, the tannin in red wines is also a part of the acid family as well. But because tannin gives wine such distinctive properties, it is generally considered a separate component in wine tasting.

MICHAEL WEISS is a professor of wine studies at the Culinary Institute of America in Hyde Park, New York. He has coauthored, with other faculty members, the textbook *Exploring Wine: The Culinary Institute of America's Complete Guide to Wines of the World* as well as the consumer guide *WineWise*. He hails from Montreal and writes about wine and food for the Hudson Valley's *Connoisseur* magazine. Weiss serves as a wine judge at home and abroad, and in 2007 he received the lifetime achievement award for education from the European Wine Council.

- **ACIDITY IS PERCEIVED ON CONTACT WITH TASTE BUDS, CREATING AN INSTANTANEOUS JOLT OF TARTNESS THAT LEAVES THE TONGUE TINGLING.**

The presence of acidity can be detected by scent, but it is most apparent as a taste sensation when we sip a beverage. It is felt as an immediate "zing," which is often most vivid down the sides of the tongue, as occurs when you sip lemonade. Acidity triggers salivation, which causes the mouth to water. Humans are highly sensitive to acidity and can detect its presence at 1 part per 130,000, as compared to 1 part per 200 for sweetness.

- **ALL WINES ARE HIGH IN ACIDITY BUT WILL VARY BY GRAPE VARIETY AND GEOGRAPHY.**

Some grape varieties are known for their acidity; Pinot Noir, for example, is more acidic than Zinfandel. As a broad generalization, acidity tends to decrease as fruit ripens and becomes sweeter. Ripening is driven by sunshine and warmth, so a correlation often exists between climate and acidity; the coolest wine regions produce the most highly acidic wines. Since sugar in ripe grapes is the source of alcohol and sugars rise as acids fall, wines with the lowest alcohol content often tend to be high in acidity.

- **ACIDITY PROVIDES A REFRESHING SENSATION AND BALANCES OTHER WINE COMPONENTS, SUCH AS ALCOHOL AND SWEETNESS.**

Sometimes called wine's "backbone," acidity is an important structural element of wine, as are alcohol and tannin. Wine's acidity also acts as a natural preservative, helping wines to age gracefully. Without acidity, wine would not taste refreshing; it would seem dull and flabby, like a shot of flavored vodka in a glass of water. Acid is especially critical in sweet wines. If you compared two dessert wines with identical sugar content, the one with lower acidity would seem more cloying, whereas the one balanced with high acidity would seem less sugary and brighter in flavor as well.

ACIDITY LEVELS OF COMMON WINE STYLES

Low	**White:** Chardonnay (Popular California), Viognier **Red:** Merlot, Zinfandel, Petite Sirah **Dessert/Fortified:** Cream Sherry, Muscat, Vin Santo
Medium	**White:** Pinot Grigio, Chardonnay (French), Fumé Blanc **Red:** Cabernet Sauvignon, Shiraz, Bordeaux, Rioja **Dessert/Fortified:** Sauternes, Port
High	**Sparkling:** Champagne, Prosecco, Cava **White:** Sauvignon Blanc, Riesling, Chenin Blanc **Red:** Pinot Noir, Burgundy, Chianti, Barolo, Barbera **Dessert/Fortified:** Icewine, Madeira, Tokaji Aszu, Auslese

- **A WINE'S TEMPERATURE DRAMATICALLY AFFECTS THE PERCEPTION OF ITS ACIDITY.**

Wine's acidity is one reason that proper service temperature is vitally important. When wine is too warm, its alcohol and acidity combine in an unpleasant way; the wine-tasting term *hot* refers to the mild "burn" of such volatile vapors more than to actual temperature. When served too cold, wine's acids and aromatic components become difficult to discern, and the wine will seem flat and flavorless.

- **WINE'S ACIDITY BLOCKS THE PERCEPTION OF SALTINESS IN FOOD, A MAJOR REASON THAT WINE IS SO FOOD-FRIENDLY.**

Perceptions of acid and salt neutralize each other. Thanks to a quirk of tongue physiology, wine's initial impression of sourness is dramatically reduced after a single bite of salty food such as cheese or smoked salmon. The reverse is also true; food will seem less salty after a sip of tangy wine. Although temporary, the effect is central to wine and food pairings. Since most foods are at least mildly salty, wine will almost always taste less acidic with food than it does alone.

INSIDER TIP: In most cases, dry wines need to taste a little too acidic on first sip in order to taste just right with food. Beginners often find dry wines to be harshly acidic on first impression, especially classic European styles, like Champagne, Sancerre, and Chianti. On first sip, such high-acid wines can seem austere, especially when they're also very dry. However, these wines were not designed to taste best alone; rather, they were designed with highly salted food in mind.

MARNIE'S CORNER

Acidity is a critical component in wine. It is responsible for much of what makes wine superior to other beverages as a food partner. Yet the sword cuts both ways. Acidity is also a characteristic that leads wine to disappoint many inexperienced drinkers on first sip. It is at least partially responsible for wine's unfortunate reputation as an "acquired taste."

Wine's acidity is usually most intense on the first impression, and it may seem unpleasantly mouth-puckering at first. On second sip, this shocking tartness tends to soften. When foods high in salt or acids enter the mix, each subsequent sip will seem even less acidic. Classic wine styles were meant to be judged at the table, as food partners, not alone. Since many wines seem overly sour on first sip, beginners may decide that they don't like the style or, worse, that they don't like wine.

HOW TO ASSESS BODY IN WINE

(AND WHY IT MATTERS)

DAVID RAMEY
Winemaker

WINE'S BODY IS part of the bedrock when it comes to tasting; it is one of the defining characteristics of style. Body plays a major role in personal preferences and is the single most important factor to consider in complementing food. Yet confusion abounds about what body is and what it isn't. It can be both obvious and elusive. From a single sip almost anyone can tell you whether a wine is light or full in body, but few could tell you how they know.

Body is texture. It is a tactile sensation of thickness sometimes referred to as "weight" or "strength." Body is a single characteristic on the mental tasting checklist, but it often varies in proportion with others, such as flavor intensity or depth of color. Wine grapes, regions, and styles are associated with degrees of body as well. Because body is so central and connected to everything else, learning how it works can help the novice make sense of wine. It can even help to roughly predict a wine's style before we open the bottle.

DAVID RAMEY is one of a select group of winemakers credited with revolutionizing modern-day California wine by bringing European traditions back to the New World. Trained at the University of California at Davis, Ramey was later introduced to time-honored French methods of making wines of unique distinction during a stint working at Bordeaux's renowned Château Pétrus. He helped establish a number of top California wineries, including Chalk Hill, Matanzas Creek, Dominus Estate, and Rudd Estate, before founding his own Ramey Wine Cellars in 1996 with his wife, Carla, in Sonoma's Healdsburg.

- **BODY IS A TACTILE SENSATION, NOT A TASTE OR A SMELL.**
  We feel body as wine's texture through the sense of touch on the palate, often called "mouthfeel." What we perceive as body is essentially "viscosity." Just as cream feels thicker than skim milk, wine is more viscous than water. Other indicators of body are the slow-moving "tears" that form and fall down the sides of the glass when we swirl a full-bodied wine. But we use the term *body* exclusively to refer to the way a wine feels in the mouth—its texture, thickness, or viscosity.

- **THERE ARE TWO MAIN SOURCES OF BODY IN WINE: ALCOHOL AND SUGAR.**
  Alcohol feels thicker in the mouth than water. Where a sip of water feels delicate, vodka feels rich. In most cases alcohol content determines a wine's body: the higher the alcohol, the more full-bodied the wine feels. There is only one other major body-building component in wine, which is less often a factor. Wines with significant residual sugar, such as dessert wines, will also feel palpably thick, similar to the way maple syrup feels. This is thanks to their "dry extract," the sum of solids that remain if wine's liquid were boiled away. In addition to any residual sugar, this dry extract typically includes trace amounts of acids, minerals, phenols, and tannins.

- **NORMAL, MEDIUM-BODIED WINE IS NOW APPROXIMATELY 13.5 PERCENT ALCOHOL.**
  Alcohol content is required on all wine labels and is usually tucked in the small print. Among dry wines, we can safely use this information to predict wine's body. Wines with less than 13 percent alcohol will seem progressively lighter; those over 14 percent will feel progressively fuller, or heavier.

- **BODY IS DIRECTLY CONNECTED TO SUNSHINE AND RIPENESS, AND THEREFORE TO A VINEYARD'S CLIMATE.**
  The sweetest grapes make the most full-bodied wines; sugar is the raw material for producing alcohol. The warmest, sunniest wine regions are those that grow the ripest, sweetest fruit. Warm and sunny wine regions, such as those of California and

Australia, will always produce more full-bodied wines. Wines from cooler, cloudier regions, namely northern France or Germany, will always be more light-bodied.

- **SOME GRAPE VARIETIES ARE SWEETER THAN OTHERS, SO THEY MAKE MORE FULL-BODIED WINES.**
  Just as pink grapefruits get sweeter than white ones, some grape varieties naturally become sweeter too. Among whites, Chardonnay and Viognier are more full-bodied on average than Sauvignon Blanc and Pinot Grigio; Riesling and Albariño are lighter still. Less diversity in body is found among reds since light-bodied reds aren't commercially popular. However, grapes like Cabernet Sauvignon, Shiraz, Zinfandel, and Nebbiolo are those most likely to have higher than average alcohol.

- **FULL-BODIED WINE IS OFTEN MISTAKENLY EQUATED WITH HIGH-QUALITY WINE.**
  There is a kernel of truth here, but it's not as simple as it appears. Body, and the factors that create it, produce effects that reach beyond texture alone. Alcohol evaporates more easily than water, boosting perceptions of aroma and flavor. Ripeness develops potent grape flavor and deepens color. Back when all fine wine came from cool zones in Europe, the warmest summers and sunniest vineyards and sweetest grapes were those that made the best wines—the richest, fullest, darkest, and most aromatic wines. But, body alone doesn't make a wine great, and it is more appropriate for some styles than others. Think about football players. A big, strong defensive lineman is not a better player than the quarterback. Likewise, a wine's strength needs to be appropriate to its style, to the role it plays. It is natural to admire fine, full-bodied wines, but many world-class wines are medium-bodied or light-bodied.

MARNIE'S CORNER

Body may be the most important factor in choosing wine. Wines that are more light-bodied feel more refreshing, so we crave them in warm weather. The reverse is true for more full-bodied styles, whose heart-warming qualities we hanker for in colder months. We're most likely to want to start off with light wines as aperitifs to pique the appetite, opting to serve the heaviest wines with the main dish. Most important, our perception of body as wine's texture correlates closely with how we perceive texture in food. Alcohol feels rich in the mouth in almost exactly the same way as fat does. The more oils or fats in a particular dish, the better it will harmonize with full-bodied, high-alcohol wines.

HOW TO GET A GRIP ON
TANNIN IN RED WINES

ZELMA LONG
Winemaker

TANNIN IS AN essential wine component, associated most strongly with red wines. It often gets a bad rap because we notice it most when it's least pleasant. Tannins are responsible for the distinctive mouth-drying astringency of red wine and can be problematic when consumed with some types of food. In poorly made wines, tannin can contribute coarse, bitter, or harsh qualities. But tannin is also a critical building block in winemaking; without it, fine red wines would lose their velvety texture and remarkable ability to age well. Tannin provides wine with structure, just as your skeleton supports your body. Best of all, the documented health benefits of drinking red wine come thanks to compounds like tannin.

Tannin is a member of an important group of wine compounds called phenolics that occur naturally in plants to help protect them against environmental dangers. Potent antioxidants, they counteract everything from insects to ultraviolet rays. They are found where self-defense is most critical, the point at which a plant meets the world (tree bark, for example). Wine tannins come from the skins of red grapes, though grape stems, seeds, and even oak barrels contribute minor amounts as well. And just

ZELMA LONG is one of the foremost women in the world of wine. One of the first women to study enology and viticulture at the University of California at Davis, she began her winemaking career at Robert Mondavi Winery, where she rose to lead the winemaking team as they came into prominence. Long later went on to lead Sonoma's Simi Winery and has been a partner in Napa Valley's Long Vineyards for more than 30 years. Currently, she and her husband, Phil Freese, grow and make Vilafonte wines Series C and Series M in an innovative joint winery and vineyard venture in the Cape of South Africa. Long also consults on winemaking internationally.

as tannins protect plants, they also protect wine. They act as powerful preservatives, slowing the oxidation that degrades wine over time.

Managing tannins is one of a winemaker's most important tasks, and a real challenge since their complex behavior is not yet fully understood. Fortunately, wine drinkers needn't master biochemistry to pick up a few useful insights regarding tannin in wine. Learning a little about where it comes from and how we perceive it, as well as how it changes with age and in the presence of food, can help you become a more confident red wine lover.

- **TANNIN COMES PRIMARILY FROM GRAPE SKINS, WHICH ARE USED ONLY IN MAKING RED WINES.**
  Because grape juice and pulp are colorless, making red wine requires extraction of the color from dark grape skins into the wine. The warmth and complex chemical reactions of fermentation help accomplish this, boosted by frequent mixing of solids and liquid. Only red wines are so strongly "skin-driven." Grape skin components such as tannins and other phenolics define them in every way—in color, flavor, aromatics, and texture ("mouthfeel"). Other styles either discard grape skins from the start, such as white wines and sparkling wines, or quickly curtail their influence, as for pink rosé wines.

- **TANNIN IS A TACTILE COMPONENT OF WINE'S "MOUTHFEEL," PERCEIVED AS A LINGERING PHYSICAL SENSATION OF DRYNESS.**
  The effect can range from a faint and pleasant fuzzy feeling, similar to biting into a perfect peach, to an aggressive sapping of saliva, as if someone wiped the inside of your mouth dry with a paper towel. In wine tasting, tannin is perceived as almost entirely tactile; we describe the way tannin feels in the mouth, not how it tastes or smells. Depending on the ripeness of the grape tannins and the amount present, tannin provides a range of textures, from "drying" to "round and smooth" to "velvety."

- **TANNINS ACT AS NATURAL ANTIOXIDANT PRESERVATIVES, AFFECTING HOW RED WINES DEVELOP AND CHANGE WITH AGE.**
Without tannin, red wine would quickly fall apart, as occurs with low-tannin Beaujolais wines that taste best when young and fresh. The protective aspects of tannins put the brakes on natural deterioration, a process dominated by oxidation. Tannins, like other natural wine compounds, will change slowly with time, often yielding "softer" wines. High-tannin reds are best able to withstand the test of time; one example is Cabernet Sauvignon, a grape whose small berries and thick skins yield high tannin content.

- **DEPTH OF COLOR WAS ONCE A GOOD PREDICTOR OF TANNIN, BUT NOT ANYMORE.**
Many people assume that the darkest wines will be the most tannic, but this rule of thumb no longer holds true. Centuries ago, longevity was prized. The best wines needed to be dark and flavorful to age well, and those types of wines were often high in tannic astringency as well. Wines with such strong skin character were harsh in youth but softened and mellowed with years in the bottle. Although overall flavor intensity fades with time, tannin preserves wine long enough for new layers of aromatic complexity to develop, as they do in aged cheeses. The most tannic red wines—fine French Bordeaux, for example—might have taken ten years or more to reach their peak. However, the market no longer wants longevity. In fact, quite the opposite is true. Since the market wants instant gratification, winemakers have learned how to make a red wine flavorful and richly colored with soft "velvety" tannins, more ready to drink on release. Today you're unlikely to encounter sky-high tannins even in wines as dark as ink.

MARNIE'S CORNER

Winespeak is notoriously obtuse, and the confusion surrounding the meaning and use of *dry* serves as the perfect example. Even though high-tannin wines literally "dry out" the mouth, we don't call them *dry* wines. Instead, that term is reserved to describe the absence of sweetness in wine. So we're left groping for other words to describe tannin's drying effects. We might describe a juicy Shiraz or other wine with mild tannin as "soft," "velvety," or "plush." Wines with stronger tannin might be called "firm" or "structured," or in extreme cases even overtly "tannic" or "tight," as with young Cabernet Sauvignon. In a strangely appropriate metaphor, tannin character may be referred to as "grip," and sometimes it really does feel like the wine has taken hold of the flesh in your mouth and won't let go.

HOW TO JUDGE WHETHER
A WINE IS "GOOD"

TRACI DUTTON
Sommelier & Wine Educator

PEOPLE ARE HIGHLY conscious that wines vary in quality. Terms such as *good wine* and *bad wine* are thrown around in a way that is not seen with most other agricultural products or food items. The perceived quality issue compounds the difficulty of choosing a wine and is yet another source of consternation for many wine consumers. No one wants to be the sucker stuck drinking the "bad wine." Most would prefer that their wine choices reflect well on them.

Great wine is a sensual pleasure that's easy to recognize but hard to describe. Even so, many wine drinkers don't feel confident in their ability to assess quality. Prices and scores are treated as being more authoritative than first-hand experience, and often a form of wine-related peer pressure plays a role as well. Recently, a comment by a student from upstate New York drove this point home for me. Speaking of wines from her local Finger Lakes region, known for off-dry white wines, the young lady said in an exaggerated way, "They are just *not good*." I don't think her judgment was really based on wine quality; vineyards in the Finger Lakes produce world-class Rieslings, among the best in the country. She meant instead that these wines lack *prestige*, that low alcohol and slight sweetness banish

TRACI DUTTON serves as sommelier for the Culinary Institute of America at Greystone, the Napa Valley outpost of the nation's most respected cooking school based in Hyde Park, New York. She is responsible for managing every aspect of the beverage program at the California campus, from purchasing and pairing menus to the CIA's Professional Wine Studies Program. Her wine lists and imaginative "Flights of Fancy" have garnered many awards. She frequently acts as a judge at wine competitions and is the contributing wine writer for the first Greystone focused cookbook on seasonal wine country cuisine.

them from polite wine society. Unfortunately, her novice's perspective on the question of good and bad in wine is fairly widespread.

So, what is "good wine"? How do professionals assess quality? Judging a wine's quality has nothing to do with personal preferences. The sommelier must have on hand something for everyone, just as the pastry chef must cover all the confectionary bases, from key lime pie to chocolate cake. Here's a peek at what we in the business look for and how we distinguish between simply *good* and truly *excellent* when it comes to wine.

- ## FIRST, WE VERIFY THAT A WINE ISN'T ACTUALLY "BAD," THAT IT IS SOUND AND WITHOUT OBVIOUS FLAWS.

  All sorts of things can go wrong with wine, from the vineyard to the winery and from the store to your glass. Looking at the bottle or sniffing the cork will not help; the best thing is to smell the wine in the glass. Does it smell appetizing? Most defects make themselves known by their "off" smells, whether the problem is microbiological spoilage or exposure to extreme heat. It's one thing if the smell of the wine reminds you of cheese or leather; those can be pleasant accents. But if it reeks of mildew or vinegar, that could signal trouble. Trust your gut. If a little voice in your head is telling you not to put the wine in your mouth, there's probably a fault or flaw present. Today these problems are rare, but, if present, the wine can justifiably be called "bad."

- ## NEXT, WE MAKE SURE THE WINE IS "GOOD," MEANING THAT IT IS WELL MADE AND APPROPRIATE FOR ITS GRAPE AND REGION.

  "Well made" just means serviceable—that the wine does what it's supposed to do. To determine this aspect, it's useful to know what qualities are expected from the particular style of wine. White wine should be refreshing; red wine should be flavorful; sparkling wine should have bubbles; dessert wine should be sweet; and so on. Whether a wine is made properly involves many varied technical factors, but you need not know how to make wine to decide if it was done right. At the most basic level, if a wine is free of faults and tastes like its style should taste, then it is a good wine. As your abilities develop, look to reliable sources to help you understand a range of suitable smells and flavors for major types of grapes and places and add these to your mental rolodex of wine.

- **WHEN TRYING TO DECIDE IF A WINE IS BETTER THAN GOOD—IF IT IS SUPERIOR OR EVEN OUTSTANDING—WE PAY ATTENTION TO THE WINE'S FINISH, OR AFTERTASTE.**

Great wines stand out from the everyday, just as the feel of cashmere stands out in a pile of wool sweaters. The finest combine desirable tastes, scents, and textures in a pleasant lingering known as the finish, that lasts long after we swallow. Whether the wine is as whisper light as French Champagne or as dark and brooding as Napa Valley Cabernet, the intensity and duration of the finish is one of the best ways to judge quality. Think of it like stemware. Everyday wineglasses are inexpensive and mass produced. When we toast with them, they make a short, disappointing "clink." But those made of fine crystal are more refined and luxurious. When two crystal glasses meet, the sound is musical and hangs in the air like a silver bell. In much the same way, the best wines resonate on the palate after each sip, whereas modest ones fade quickly. Generally, the longer the finish, the higher the quality. The greatest wines will move us personally, in the same way as an artistic masterpiece.

MARNIE'S CORNER

There is an unfortunate tendency among wine novices to doubt their own judgment and to adopt preferences modeled by others. But different people perceive wines differently, so what's delicious to one may be uninspiring to another. It's also true that our tastes in wine change with time and experience. At the beginning of our wine lives, most of us favor styles that have an obvious fruitlike flavor or even noticeable sweetness. An appreciation for mature wines, earthy wines, and very dry wines tends to be an acquired taste. But no one should feel pressured to pretend they like something they don't, especially if the wines they really prefer are simpler and less expensive.

CHAPTER
THREE

Wine Shopping

FOR MANY WINE LOVERS, THE RETAIL SHOPPING EXPERIENCE IS BITTERSWEET. WE KNOW THE STORE IS FILLED WITH DELICIOUS TREASURES, BUT WE CAN'T ALWAYS figure out which bottle holds the one we crave. And like the proverbial box of chocolates, there's only one way to find out what you're going to get. In most cases, tasting a wine before buying it isn't possible.

Very few wine stores are legally able to offer samples, and many don't have knowledgeable salespeople available to assist. The feeling of helplessness that wine shopping can trigger has few parallels in the world of retail shopping. We can evaluate whether a shirt suits our style or whether a tomato looks healthy and ripe. We can try on shoes and test drive cars to get a sense of whether they meet our needs. With wine, a surprising number of shoppers feel so overwhelmed that they take stabs in the dark, basing their decision on factors as arbitrary as label art.

But, there are simple steps you can take to improve your odds of finding a wine you'll like. Where you choose to shop will greatly impact your options. Learn which bits of label information provide the most insight and which are best tuned out. Most of all, plan your priorities. A strategy that works for finding reliable premium wines won't help if you're shopping for value.

HOW TO GET STARTED
IN WINE STORES

MADELINE TRIFFON
Master Sommelier

SHOPPING FOR WINE in a retail store is quite different from browsing a wine list. For starters, you're standing up! No cocktail to sip on, no bread to munch, and, most important, no helpful server or full-fledged sommelier to point you in delicious directions. So where to begin?

For starters, remain calm when faced with a wall of unfamiliar wines. No, you are not stupid; wine pros don't recognize everything either! When you walk in, take a moment to figure out how the wines are organized. Is it by country, varietal, price point, or style?

Carry a notepad and scribble notes as you browse. Much like looking through a large wine list, it's easy to forget which bottles looked promising in the first aisle by the time you make it to the back of the store. Here are some more tips to keep in mind when you head out wine shopping.

• **DETERMINE YOUR BUDGET BEFORE YOU START SHOPPING.**
Budgeting a dollar amount per bottle will allow you to zero in on wines you can afford. Firmly understand that you don't have to spend more than you are comfortable

Master sommelier **MADELINE TRIFFON** serves as director of wine for the Matt Prentice Restaurant Group based in Detroit. In 1987 she became one of only two female master sommeliers in the world at that time, and only the eighth American to join their ranks. She enthusiastically mentors the next generation of sommeliers and currently serves on the board of the American Chapter of the Court of Master Sommeliers. Her wine lists have garnered countless awards, and *Santé* magazine named her their Wine and Spirits Professional of the Year for 1999. In 2008 Triffon received the "Women Who Inspire Award" from Women Chefs and Restauranteurs (WCR).

with. Ten to fifteen dollars will buy a good bottle of wine. Premium wines can be defined as costing more than $30 a bottle. View these as special occasion wines or as selections to share with wine-savvy friends and guests. If shopping for multiple bottles for a party, remember that every dollar below your target can be used toward another bottle!

- **TO DISCOVER THE BEST VALUES, PAY ATTENTION TO FEATURED ITEMS: DISCOUNTED STACKS, EMPLOYEE PICKS, SALE BINS, AND AISLE-END DISPLAYS.**
  For killer buys, the bins in the front of the store are your best bet. These may include "highly recommended" wines that the store has recently purchased or fine wines that are on sale to make room for new vintages.

- **IF ASSISTANCE IS AVAILABLE, TAKE ADVANTAGE OF IT.**
  Not all wine shops have knowledgeable staff, but those that do offer such service care most about directing their customers. Look to younger staff for enthusiasm; seek mature staff for depth of knowledge. Ask if the wine buyer is available for recommendations or to provide weekly picks. Be direct and expressive about what you're looking for, what you like, the amount you can spend, and for what occasion the wine is intended.

- **IF YOU'RE ON YOUR OWN, CLOSELY EXAMINE THE LABELS.**
  A wine's brand and region are always marked, and most labels indicate the grape variety too. Climate dictates style, to a large degree. Wines from cool climate regions such as Oregon tend to be lighter and have more acidity than those from sunnier, warmer places like California, which is known for fuller wines that are riper in flavor. Read the small print: Higher alcohol suggests fuller body and bolder flavor. Be sure to scan the back label as well, for these often contain a font of information, from style descriptions to food pairings.

  Though their tradition is to name wines for the region, many European wineries have started naming the grapes used as well, though this information is often tucked away on the back label. Among blends, the first grape listed is usually (but not always) the dominant one. Learning a little winemaking lingo goes a long way too: barrel-fermented, sur lies aging, malolactic. These words indicate a style. As a safe generalization, be wary of cartoony animals on the label. They usually dress the most mass-produced wines—clean but rarely notable.

Look for the names of producers whose wines you've enjoyed in the past. Much like a chef preparing food, the person behind the wine determines the style and quality. It's fun to try their wares at different price points.

M ARNIE'S CORNER

It's easy to forget what you came for when you're at the wine store, so get organized. To shop with a clear sense of purpose, make a list before you go. Determine how many bottles you need and in which general styles. Shop first for what you need most, since it's easy to lose focus. Your shopping list does not need to be specific; if you know your favorite brand of Pinot Grigio, great, or you can just write "red wine for lasagna" or "something new under $12." If a staff member offers to help you find something, you'll know exactly what to say. That shopping list will come in handy, doubling as a notepad too, so bring a pen. Jotting down each contender as you shop helps clarify your options and saves you time.

HOW TO RELATE TO YOUR
WINE RETAILER

ROBERT KACHER
Wine Importer

EVERY COMMUNITY HAS different kinds of wine stores. Some are dedicated specialists that stock only wines and spirits; others are more utilitarian, such as grocery or discount stores that offer a section dedicated to wine. Even among wine-specific retailers, you can find both giant warehouses with everything under the sun and teeny storefronts featuring a narrow, carefully curated selection. In some states, only standardized government-run state stores can sell wine. But chances are, you probably have several options.

Unfortunately, wine doesn't lend itself as easily to do-it-yourself shopping as other goods. It remains one of the thorny frontiers of retail where helpful, skilled salespeople are truly invaluable. The best place to shop for wine is a place where the staff cares about wine and is available to help. Your best wine shopping resource will always be retailers who know their wares.

When I first became interested in wine, it was considered unwise to trust wine retailers completely. The perception was that their job was to separate customers from their cash. A lot has changed over the last few decades. Americans drink more wine and are savvier shoppers; international wine quality is improving by leaps

ROBERT "BOBBY" KACHER is a high-profile importer of French wines based in Washington, D.C. He discovered a lifestyle of wine, food, and family, as well as the vineyards and kitchens of France, while backpacking in Europe during his sophomore year summer break. The lifestyle captivated him, and it grew to become an all-consuming passion. Upon returning to the United States, he worked first in retail and importing before launching his own Robert Kacher Selections in 1985. He specializes in distinctive hand-crafted French wines and has earned rave reviews for his portfolio's remarkable values.

and bounds. And there's no question that the wine shopping experience is growing ever more competitive. Wine retailers know they will survive only if customers return for more. Confidence in their choices and recommendations is the first step toward earning a loyal clientele. These days, trust in retailers is rarely misplaced.

- **DIFFERENT TYPES OF WINE STORES SERVE DIFFERENT NEEDS.**
Determining which retailer will be best for you depends on your individual priorities. For convenience, it might be the wine aisle at the supermarket, where you can pick up a bottle while deciding what's for dinner. For the steepest discounts, it might be the big-box discount club, where you can find some pedigreed wines at fire-sale prices. If you're new to wine and want to explore new styles, you'll be best served at a wine store, where the selection, service, and even the signage are all organized with the aim of helping you find the best bottle of wine.

- **WHEN YOU'RE ON YOUR OWN, TAILOR YOUR SHOPPING APPROACH TO THE TYPE OF STORE.**
There's nothing wrong with grabbing a bottle of wine at the supermarket or corner store while running errands or picking up a case on a whim while bargain hunting at the discount club. But neither venue is likely to have sales staff available to help you find what you want. You'll need to be self-sufficient, so strategize accordingly.

Supermarkets and convenience stores tend to focus on the best-known brands, and few have space to organize their shelves coherently. Turnover on obscure items can be slow in these venues, so they are not great places to experiment with lesser-known styles. Stick to grapes and regions you know and like, and to brands you're comfortable with.

Big discount chains and box stores often get extraordinary deals on bulk purchases of wine, but the selection tends to be narrow and includes wines from off the beaten track. Under these circumstances, your best bet is to keep an open mind and try one bottle first. If you like it, spring for a case quickly before it disappears from the shelves.

- **WHERE RETAIL STAFF ARE ON HAND, IT'S WORTH ASKING FOR THEIR RECOMMENDATIONS.**

  When in a wine-centric store, ask if a staff member is available to answer questions. Often that person will be quite young. You might suppose they have hardly enough experience to be a fountain of wine lore. But today wine information and tasting experience are easier than ever to access, and we are seeing the emergence of an extraordinarily well educated generation of wine professionals. Many are well traveled, and most are dedicated to pleasing the customer. So seek out their insights, trust their recommendations, and put yourself in their hands. Don't be shy about discussing your budget or sharing wines you've enjoyed in the past. The worst that can happen is that you might discover you don't share their tastes. But if the sales staff at your local wine shop are good at what they do, they should be able to help you discover a world of new wine experiences, one bottle at a time.

- **KEEP AN OPEN MIND AND DON'T READ TOO MUCH INTO WINE SCORES.**

  If the salesperson at your local store is talking up a wine, that is reason enough to try it. Media figures certainly have extensive expertise and are professional and credible, but their tastes might not be in synch with yours. Your retailer will be more attuned to context, able to adapt to the seasons and availability. They can also inquire about your lifestyle and food habits to offer personalized advice. At the end of the day, the critics may have great skill, but they have no stake in your wine-shopping transaction. Your retailer, however, has not only more information about you but also some skin in the game—a built-in market-driven incentive to make you happy.

MARNIE'S CORNER

Wine is a remarkably diverse product by nature, an agri-cultural commodity that has thousands of producers and more variations than any one store could possibly stock. We have a tendency to judge a wine store by the size of its selection, but this can be a misleading metric. Often the very best wine stores are those with a small, but carefully selected roster of offerings. In these circumstances, it's more likely that each and every wine has been vetted thoroughly and that each wine fills a stylistic need. So, don't judge quality by quantity—wait until you've tried a few of their wines before deciding whether or not to go back. In fact, asking for a mixed case of recommendations is a great way to get a handle on whether or not your retailer is up to snuff.

HOW TO GUESSTIMATE
WINE STYLE FROM
PACKAGING CLUES

OLIVIA BORU
Sommelier

I T'S A CLASSIC scene: You head into the wine shop, feeling adventurous, ready to try something different. Instead of the same old bottle, you pick up the next one. But something on the label has you scratching your head.

"Why does it say 'old vines'? Hmm . . . is 'old' a good thing for vines to be? Okay, let's try the next one . . . this one says 'Saralee's Vineyard.' Saralee who? Is this wine supposed to go with pastries?"

Risk takers may take a chance on an unfamiliar new wine, but many will wander back to the comfort of that familiar—but boring—old friend.

Wine labels can be impenetrable for the uninitiated. What other food presents us with labels that communicate so little about how the product will taste? Being a savvy wine shopper requires an awful lot of homework. Between all the grapes and all the regions, all the hierarchies and all the styles, it's tempting just to give up and buy vodka. Some people find it fun, like a gastronomic trivia game. But for most, the idea of studying just to go wine shopping is a total buzz-kill.

OLIVIA BORU is a sommelier and wine educator in Baltimore, Maryland. As sommelier for Tony Foreman and Cindy Wolf's collection of restaurants, she divides her time among some of the finest establishments in the city, including Charleston, Pazo, Petit Louis Bistro, and Cinghiale, each boasting an award-winning wine list. Known for her easy-to-understand approach to wine education, Boru works to demystify the complex world of fine wine for her guests and students.

Classic wine labels *typically feature family names in elegant script on light backgrounds. Imagery will be old-fashioned in execution and subject matter.*

Don't fret though, there's hope for you yet. Even if varietals and appellations don't ring a bell, wine bottles and labels can still be your guide. Think of it as traveling in a country where you don't speak the language—you'd be amazed what you can figure out from body language and tone of voice without understanding a word. In wine, the package holds clues to style that can help you guess what's in the bottle without pulling the cork.

- **ALCOHOL CONTENT IS ALWAYS PRINTED ON THE LABEL AND IS A RELIABLE INDICATOR OF BALLPARK WINE STYLE.**
  By law, alcohol content must be declared on the label, and it is a terrific clue for predicting wine style. Because sugar becomes alcohol during winemaking, alcoholic strength tells you roughly how ripe and sweet the grapes were, a factor that has implications for overall flavor and acidity. The norm for alcoholic strength among

Modern wine labels may incorporate humorous names, modern graphics, bright colors, or even cartoon characters.

modern wines is approximately 13.5 percent. High-alcohol wines are strong and full-bodied; they're typically bold in flavor as well. Low-alcohol wines are more light-bodied and frequently more tangy, too. If the alcohol is unusually low, less than 11.5 percent, you can be virtually certain that the wine is a little sweet, since at least some grape sugar was not fully converted into alcohol.

- **LABEL ART AND PACKAGE DESIGN PROVIDE INSIGHTS INTO BOTH A VINTNER'S SENSIBILITIES AND THE TARGET AUDIENCE.**
  Chances are, you already knew this, but let me just confirm it: Wines whose labels are decorated with cartoon characters are being marketed to a different clientele than those featuring dignified engravings of stately châteaux. Wineries are highly conscious of how their bottles look and to whom they appeal. Although the following assessments are sweeping generalizations, they do reflect trends in the marketplace. Jokey

wine names and cartoon critters are aimed squarely at beginners looking for an "ice-breaker"; think vivid fruity flavors and maybe even subliminal sweetness. Colorful, creative, or modern-looking labels that are more style conscious than cutesy are more often found on sleek wines made in the fruit-forward genre popular in New World regions such as California and Chile. In theory, classic label designs—simple script on white background with a discreet crest or winery scene—suggest Old World sophistication, meaning food orientation and finesse. However, since traditional labels also connote prestige, they are widely imitated and therefore less reliable indicators of style. They are found on everything from "Two Buck Chuck" to Château Lafite-Rothschild.

- **UNCOMMON PACKAGING SPEAKS VOLUMES: SCREW TOPS, EXTRA-HEAVY BOTTLES FOR REDS, CLEAR GLASS FOR WHITES.**
  Any vintner who's willing to take the plunge into high-tech packaging, such as stelvin-lined screw tops instead of classic corks, is likely to favor modern over old-fashioned wine style. You can expect vibrant, clean, fruit-driven flavor and are less likely to find earthy or rustic character. Super-thick glass gives bottles more durability and heft, but they cost a lot more as well, and so they are most often used for dense and long-lived reds that aspire to greatness. Historically, wine bottles have been dark brown or dark green to shield the contents from damaging light. However, since clear glass makes white wine look more refreshing, image-conscious wineries are lightening up the bottles. The clearer the glass, the more likely it is to hold a midweight dry white with citrusy or apple-y flavors, along the lines of Sauvignon Blanc or Pinot Grigio.

MARNIE'S CORNER

Packaging can provide clues to whether we're looking at a modern or traditional wine. But what does that translate to in the glass? Overall, old-school winemaking favors food orientation over first impressions. On first sip such wines are likely to seem a little sharp, earthy, or thin but shine at the table as food partners. Compared to the norm, we may find them to be drier and lighter bodied, often with higher acidity and subtler flavor. Modern wines are typically more polished, designed to make a wholly positive first impression of ripe fruit. They generally present more squeaky-clean aromas but may lack individuality. Compared to the traditional style, they are often less dry and more full-bodied.

HOW TO DECIDE WHICH WINES ARE READY TO DRINK

JANCIS ROBINSON
Master of Wine & Wine Author

W INE, LIKE ALL food products, changes over time. Unlike most agricultural commodities, however, it has the potential to resist deterioration and to improve with age. Defiance of time, an implacable force of nature, has for centuries been one of wine's most distinctive features and a source of great admiration.

A belief that all wine ages well is widespread, but in truth very few do. The vast majority are designed to taste best upon release from the winery, and many begin to lose their appeal within six months. At best, one in ten red wines may taste appreciably more interesting or pleasant after five years; among whites, this rate drops by half. Less than one in a hundred wines is likely to taste better after a decade or more, and these sorts of wines are becoming rarer by the year.

The challenge is deciding when to drink a particular wine. How can the average wine shopper recognize which to consume immediately and which to set aside? And for those to be cellared, how long must one wait? There are no clear-cut answers, but here are some general rules of thumb for determining which wines might have a great future and which are best suited for immediate consumption.

One of a handful of wine communicators with an international reputation, **JANCIS ROBINSON** writes daily for her Web site, weekly for *The Financial Times*, and bimonthly for a column syndicated on every continent. She is also editor of *The Oxford Companion to Wine* and coauthor, with Hugh Johnson, of *The World Atlas of Wine*, recognized as standard references worldwide. In 1984 she was the first person outside the wine trade to pass the rigorous Master of Wine exams. In 2003 Robinson was awarded an Order of the British Empire by Her Majesty the Queen, on whose cellar she now advises.

- **VALUE-PRICED WINES SHOULD BE CONSUMED AS FRESH AS POSSIBLE.**
The vast majority of wines are cheap, cheerful, and designed to be drunk young. The economics of producing wines to sell below $10 a bottle precludes achieving levels of concentration that might add complexity with bottle age. Most decline quickly, so drink up.

- **WINE'S POTENTIAL TO IMPROVE WITH AGE DEPENDS ON ITS COMPOSITION. GRAPE AND REGION PLAY MAJOR ROLES, BUT QUALITY IS THE CRITICAL FACTOR.**
The more flavor compounds—such as acids, phenolics, and esters—that are present in a wine at bottling, the more potential for interactions among them. Such interplay is what creates the wine's secondary scents, or bouquet. Thick-skinned grapes with the lowest water content tend to produce the most concentrated wines. Therefore, the greatest likelihood of gaining flavor interest with maturity is found in wines made from high-flavor grape varieties that received little rain or irrigation during the growing season—in short, wines of high quality. Typically, the more expensive a wine, the more likely it is to reward patient cellaring. Fine dessert wines, such as botrytised white Sauternes and fortified red Port, are exceptionally concentrated and evolve the most slowly of all.

- **WINE'S PRIMARY "FRUITY" AROMA FADES SLOWLY OVER TIME, AND VERY FEW WILL GAIN SECONDARY SCENTS, OR "BOUQUET," WITH AGE.**
To improve, a wine must acquire additional layers of aromatic complexity to offset the inevitable loss of flavor that occurs over time. Among red wines, astringent tannins that can seem harsh in youth will also soften gradually with bottle age.

- **POPULAR PREMIUM WINES ARE GENERALLY DESIGNED TO BE AT THEIR BEST ON RELEASE, REGARDLESS OF COLOR OR STYLE.**
The modern wine market's preference is for instant gratification, not for old-fashioned wines that require cellaring to taste right. As a sweeping generalization, one could say

that the more widely available a branded wine is, the more likely it is to be ready to drink upon release from the winery and not to improve significantly after one year.

- **AMONG TOP-QUALITY WINES, REDS ARE THE MOST LIKELY TO IMPROVE, WHITES DO NOT KEEP AS WELL, AND PINK ROSÉS FADE MOST QUICKLY.**

Grape skins are rich in astringent tannins and dark anthocyanins, two phenolics that help preserve wine. Over time, they merge into larger complex compounds, which are eventually precipitated as sediment. This process takes years and leaves the mature red wine paler in color and softer in mouthfeel. In general, the red wines from the thickest-skinned grapes that are darkest in youth are those most likely to make wines with the potential for long-term aging.

Because grape skins are discarded when making white wine, whites are generally lower in preservative phenolics. Instead, acidity can extend white wine's life. High-acid whites such as Riesling deteriorate much more slowly than richer whites, including Chardonnay. Rosé wines are the least stable, with most of them noticeably "tired" by the time of the next year's harvest.

AGING POTENTIAL OF COMMON WINE STYLES

Long Term	**White:** Riesling, Chenin Blanc **Red:** Cabernet Sauvignon, Nebbiolo, Syrah/Shiraz
Medium Term	**White:** Chardonnay, Grüner Veltliner, Semillon **Red:** Merlot, Pinot Noir, Tempranillo, Sangiovese, Grenache
Short Term	**White:** Sauvignon Blanc, Pinot Grigio, Viognier **Red:** Zinfandel, Gamay, Dolcetto

M ARNIE'S CORNER

Looking at all those vintages on wine labels can be intimidating. They give the impression that one should know which to choose and which to avoid. In most cases, however, it's more useful to think of them as indicators of style. Among wines released during a given year, those with the most recent vintage dates are most likely to emphasize youthful fruitiness. The youngest whites will be unoaked and full of snappy acidity, whereas the youngest reds should display a fresh and sappy charm. Older vintages will range more widely but should offer greater depth and complexity, often thanks to barrel aging at the winery.

HOW TO COMPARE CORKS AND SCREW CAPS, BOTTLES AND BOXES

MELISSA MONOSOFF
Sommelier

FOR MORE THAN a century, wine has been packaged in one way only: in a glass bottle with a wooden cork. Bottles and corks remained unchanged for decades while other types of products changed containers because, until recently, they still worked better than anything else. However, neither the bottle nor the wooden cork is problem-free, and today alternatives for both are showing up on store shelves. Glass and natural cork will certainly remain the industry standard for years to come, but after long resistance to innovation, new technology is finally shaking up the wine world, ushering in an era of modern wine packaging.

In addition to the traditional bottle, wine now comes in boxes and cans; cork stoppers may be replaced with synthetic plugs or screw tops. These alternatives address environmental concerns and quality-control issues and are designed for efficiency and practicality. Such technologies may defy long-held notions of wine, but they are nothing to be scared about. Yes, it's hard to imagine cracking open cans of sparkling wine for New Year's Eve or having the sommelier forego the corkscrew tableside and open a bottle with a swift flick of the wrist. However, once we

MELISSA MONOSOFF is one of the Philadelphia area's top wine professionals. She is the sommelier at the award-winning Savona restaurant in Gulph Mills, Pennsylvania, and serves as a consulting sommelier for the Pennsylvania Liquor Control Board, one of the world's largest purchasers of wine and spirits. A graduate of the Culinary Institute of America, she began her hospitality career as a chef before following her wine destiny. Monosoff has managed the beverage programs of top area restaurants, such as Maia, Striped Bass, and The Fountain at the Four Seasons Hotel Philadelphia.

understand what these innovations are for, many will be just as attractive as the old familiar methods, or even more so.

- **WE HAVE LONG KNOWN THAT CORKS CAN CAUSE FLAWS AND INCONSISTENCIES IN WINE'S TASTE.**

  Corks are like little wooden sponges. Punched from the bark of a tree, they are organic and porous. Since no two corks are exactly alike, they cause slight variations in the wine stored inside. But of far greater concern is the possibility that they will cause other spoilage problems. Their nooks and crannies can host pernicious microorganisms that create off-odors. Attempts to sterilize the porous wood can cause just as much harm to the wine.

  Industry sources estimate that up to 5 percent of wines are noticeably tainted by their corks. Such wines are confusingly described as being "corked." Although the degree of spoilage varies, both consumers and winemakers lose out; a wine that tastes just slightly off is almost worse for a winery's reputation than one that is clearly flawed by its cork. Cork's inconsistencies and failure rates have become a liability.

- **THE BEST ALTERNATIVE CLOSURES, LIKE STELVIN SCREW TOPS, HAVE PROVEN SAFE FOR LONG-TERM AGING.**

  Replacements for natural corks took a long time to develop. Since the finest wines can be cellared for decades, research studies were required to ensure the alternatives could hold up over time. Discreet testing showed that many options are safe enough to use. Synthetic cork-shaped plugs are serviceable in the short term and maintain the corkscrew's comforting role; you'll see them in everything from stealthy wood tones to splashy neons. Reusable glass stoppers are even better, performance-wise, but are rarely seen outside Germany. The real winners of the race to find a better closure are screw tops made with a nonreactive stelvin liner. They are capable of protecting wine as long as or longer than natural corks, a fact supported by thirty-plus years of side-by-side trials. Although this technology has its own challenges to overcome, it has proven to have few problems and is gaining wider acceptance.

Traditional Cork   *Screw Top*   *Bag-in-the-Box*

- **GLASS BOTTLES MAY NOT FAIL AS OFTEN AS CORKS, BUT MORE EFFICIENT OPTIONS ARE NOW AVAILABLE.**

  Bottles are heavy and break easily. They are not cost prohibitive but do add significantly to the weight, bulk, and fragility of wines being shipped internationally, and this cost is passed on to the consumer. Once opened, bottles make it difficult to protect wine from oxidation and spoilage. Alternatives such as boxes and cans address both economic concerns and service efficiency. They represent the next packaging revolution and are poised to change the way people worldwide shop for wine.

- **BOXES AND CANS MAY HORRIFY TRADITIONALISTS, BUT THEY ARE GROWING IN POPULARITY DUE TO UNDENIABLE ADVANTAGES.**

  Cans are lighter than glass. They are also more recyclable, less fragile, and able to protect against damaging UV rays. They are most beneficial for moderately priced sparkling wines since they deliver a single serving with fresh bubbles every time. Small boxes are efficient for similar reasons but work better for still reds and whites; they are almost like juice boxes for wine. Cases of wine boxes are significantly lighter, smaller, and more efficient to store and ship than traditional bottles.

- **THE "BAG-IN-THE-BOX" PACKAGING IS COST-EFFECTIVE, PRACTICAL, AND ABLE TO PRESERVE WINE'S FLAVOR.**

  The bag-in-the-box has been used for years for cheap and cheerful wines, but technological improvements in the polymer lining material now make this a viable package for higher-quality wines. Also known as tetra-paks or wine "casks," these large boxes contain an impermeable mylar bag in which the wine is packed. The wine is drawn from a tap, which causes the bag to shrink as the liquid exits. Since exposure to air and oxygen causes wines to deteriorate quickly, once opened, box wines can keep wine tasting fresh much longer than bottled wines. Wine in an open bottle may flatten overnight and begin to transition to vinegar within a week or so. But boxed wines can maintain vibrant flavor for weeks. Typically, these large boxes hold the equivalent of four bottles of wine but cost on average only one-half to two-thirds as much as two standard bottles. With their efficiency at protecting wine and cost-effectiveness, it's little wonder so many wineries are beginning to regard casks as the wave of the future.

MARNIE'S CORNER

Ten years ago, only cheap jug wines had screw caps. Now these non-traditional closures can be found even on pricey reserve-tier wines. Wine drinkers have been rightly confused to see the premium wine aisle invaded by screw tops, once clear indicators of a less-than-ambitious wine. But if anything, modern stelvin closures are a sign of how seriously the vintner takes wine quality. Changing from corks to screw tops requires a significant investment in new equipment; in addition, corks may look fancy, but they are actually cheaper to make. Although winemakers risk alienating customers who are suspicious of bottles without real corks, they choose to make the switch anyway to eliminate any factor that might compromise the quality or consistency of their wines. Who can argue with that reason? The use of screw tops first caught on in modern wine regions—such as Australia and New Zealand—but increasing numbers of wineries worldwide have taken note and like what they see. The transition from cork to screw top is catching on, even in bastions of traditional practices, such as Burgundy in France.

HOW TO FIND VALUES BY STEPPING OFF THE BEATEN TRACK

RON EDWARDS
Master Sommelier

BOTH WINE NOVICES and aficionados are looking for the same thing when browsing the wine store shelves: a good wine at a great price. And why not? Value for the dollar—literally, the ratio of performance to price—is how we gauge our success as shoppers. This is true for everything from groceries to real estate. Wine should be no different.

Yet we've been conditioned to think of wine as an elite beverage. People clearly feel safer buying more expensive wine, and many regard the bargains in the store as risky. When quality matters, many people fear serving the "wrong" wine or one that might reflect poorly on them as hosts. Luckily, the chances of that happening today are slim.

The wine world is evolving quickly, and more great values can be found now than ever before. In fact, the quality of modestly priced wines is at its highest level. All you need are courage to branch out and a few strategies for locating wines that perform well for the dollar. Try to think like a sommelier or a professional wine buyer. Here are some insights into how the pros scout for bargains.

RON EDWARDS is a master sommelier, one of an elite international group of premier wine and service professionals. He is an independent consultant to all levels of the wine and hospitality trade, bringing his energy and experience to myriad businesses, from importers to hotels, and leading seminars for everyday wine drinkers and corporate clients. His monthly wine club, accessible through his Web site, offers carefully chosen selections that take the risk out of buying wine. He is also active in training the next generation through the Court of Master Sommeliers.

- **FIRST, SHAKE OFF THAT FEAR OF BUYING THE "WRONG" WINE.**
  The worst that can happen is that you might not buy that same wine again. Thanks to innovations in wine technology, inexpensive wines are of a better quality than ever before. And in the competitive modern market, poorly made wines don't get very far. When bargain shopping, you're likely not risking more than the price of a fancy deli sandwich. So what's the big deal? Thinking of wines as a "social yardstick" heaps unnecessary psychological stress onto ourselves. Buying into the "you are what you drink" mindset is a surefire way to spend more on wine than is necessary and to lose out on price-to-quality ratio.

- **RESIST THE HERD INSTINCT. THE MORE POPULAR THE WINE STYLE, THE LESS LIKELY IT IS TO DELIVER GREAT VALUE.**
  Faced with bewildering options, the natural instinct is to seek refuge in familiarity: trusted brands, famous grape varieties, pedigreed regions of origin. But that is not necessarily the best way to get the most for your dollar. Remember the law of supply and demand—the more desired a product, the higher its price. The best values will always be found in categories that other people are walking past.

- **BLUE-CHIP FACTORS SUCH AS FAMOUS REGIONS AND GRAPES CAN HELP YOU DISCOVER GREAT WINES, BUT THEY WON'T HELP YOU FIND GREAT BARGAINS.**
  Wines that inspire confidence may cost more simply because they inspire confidence, not because they're better. For example, a well-made Cabernet Sauvignon from Napa Valley will command a higher price than one from a lesser known California region such as Paso Robles wine. The unfortunate flip side is that poorly made wines can coast on the reputation of credible regions and grapes. Yet if two Cabernets—one Napa and one Paso Robles—are selling for the same price, the less familiar wine will probably deliver more quality. And if there's an even less familiar Paso Robles from a less familiar grape at the same price, that wine may well deliver the best value of all. Every variable you're willing to take a chance on—grape, region, brand, vintage—can save you money. Speaking of vintage, judge them for yourself. Vintages that are not highly rated are still usually good wines, and they're frequently better priced.

- **THE ODDS OF GETTING A GREAT DEAL WILL IMPROVE IF THE WINE IS EITHER UP-AND-COMING OR UNDERAPPRECIATED.**
When bargain hunting, it pays to take a different approach, to deliberately seek out items that others shy away from. As with many things in life, the key to getting great value for your wine dollar is to open your mind; to let new ideas in and old ideas out. The following are factors that improve your chances of finding the best price-to-quality relationships.

1. **EXPLORE UNFAMILIAR WINE REGIONS.** You'll find the best deals if you stay ahead of the curve. Be the first on your block to discover Greece, Canada, Spain, and South Africa. Remember when Chilean and Australian wines first appeared in stores? They had to earn our trust by delivering exceptional value before being accepted into the "fine wine" club. Other countries are improving and even excelling, and all will follow a similar path to credibility, first tempting us with great deals to create demand and then gradually introducing finer wines.

2. **EXPLORE UNFAMILIAR GRAPE VARIETIES.** The pedigreed grapes, such as Chardonnay and Pinot Noir, have been great for centuries. But, many others have potential, too. Obscure varieties that have historically been exploited for volume, including Chenin Blanc, Grenache, Torrontes, and Zinfandel, are underestimated based on past performance alone. Given the proper respect and attention by the winemakers, however, many of these unfamiliar grapes can and do make terrific wine.

3. **REVISIT UNFASHIONABLE CLASSICS.** Many of yesteryear's classics have simply fallen out of favor. As the media pushes people toward dense powerhouse styles, lighter-bodied gems have been overlooked. Think French Beaujolais, German Riesling, and Italian Soave. But retro-chic is coming back, and people are rediscovering the joys of drinking lighter, whether it's white Muscadet or red Valpolicella.

4. **EXPERIMENT WITH ODDBALL STYLES.** A surefire way to beat the odds is to consider quirky wines that are a little "out there." Try one of Italy's sparkling reds from such grapes as Barbera or Brachetto that range from dry to sweet. Strange, yes, but delicious, too. Or how about Sherry, Spain's ugly duckling? These fortified

wines run the gamut from transparent and bone-dry to opaque and sticky-sweet, and they are undeniably some of the world's best wines available at low, low prices. Try dry rosés, bubbly dessert wines, and so on. Ask your retailer what's available for the adventurous palate.

MARNIE'S CORNER

Sommeliers are professional wine shoppers—day in and day out their job is to unearth the best values. Because wines by the glass incur the highest losses, that's where restaurant wine buyers are looking most aggressively for value. A great shortcut for staying on top of wine industry trends is to check out which wines the highest-rated restaurants are pouring by the glass. Such styles as Argentine Malbec and New Zealand Sauvignon Blanc were popular in restaurants long before they appeared on retail shelves. Keeping an eye on what leading restaurateurs are serving doesn't require dining out; many restaurants now post this information online.

HOW TO FIND THE BEST WINES BY STICKING TO THE CLASSICS

KEVIN ZRALY
Wine Educator & Author

WINES STORES CAN be great places to spend an idle afternoon. Dawdling through the aisles as you might in a bookstore is fun if you've got the time and want to explore in search of value. But if buying that "special" wine is just one of many items on the day's to-do list, you need a plan. The number of options in the average wine shop can overwhelm many shoppers. When you're faced with so many choices, it's easy to lose focus and end up wandering aimlessly, even if you thought you knew exactly what you wanted when you walked in.

As a teacher and author, I am often asked to name the "best wines." The politically correct response would be that they're all wonderful and I love them equally. But some parts of the world simply excel at making specific wine styles. Shopping within these regions will significantly increase your odds of buying something terrific, as long as you stick to the grapes and styles they do best. Here are my opinionated shortcuts to finding the best wines within six of the most popular and important fine wine categories.

KEVIN ZRALY is a legendary American wine educator and author of the bestselling book *Windows on the World Complete Wine Course*. From 1976 until 2001 he was wine director at Windows on the World, the restaurant atop the World Trade Center, where he built one of the world's largest commercial wine cellars. A gifted speaker and lively entertainer, he is also founder and sole instructor of the Windows on the World Wine School, through which he has reached nearly 20,000 students, a number that grows every year.

1. THE WORLD'S BEST REGION FOR CABERNET SAUVIGNON AND MERLOT: BORDEAUX, FRANCE

In my opinion, the top châteaux of Bordeaux make the world's finest wines, bar none. Both of these legendary grapes are native to the region, and these are the world's "original" wines made with Cabernet Sauvignon and Merlot. In fact, those made elsewhere from this variety all look to Bordeaux for their inspiration.

The best Cabernet Sauvignon–based red Bordeaux wines come from a small district called the Médoc, just north of the city of Bordeaux. The finest Merlot-based red Bordeaux wines hail from the other side of the river, especially such towns as St. Emilion and Pomerol. Whichever grape dominates the blend, the wines from the most highly regarded estates are pricey collector's items, but there are thousands of lesser-known châteaux making excellent wine in every price range.

RUNNER-UP: CALIFORNIA. Bordeaux may have a few centuries' head start, but California's Cabernet Sauvignon and Merlot wines are quickly catching up. (Blends of both made in the Bordeaux style may be named "Meritage.")

2. THE WORLD'S BEST REGION FOR CHARDONNAY AND PINOT NOIR: BURGUNDY, FRANCE

For quality, nowhere on earth makes better Pinot Noir and Chardonnay than their native Burgundy. This is where our modern concept of fine wine was born almost one thousand years ago, and the commitment to making exceptional and expressive wines runs deep in this region. Since only a small amount of wine is made, limited availability and high prices are the main drawbacks. In general, value is more easily found in white Burgundies than in red ones.

RUNNERS-UP: CALIFORNIA AND OREGON (PINOT NOIR). American interpretations of the Burgundian style are very good. They tend to be richer and more fruit driven than the French icons on which they're modeled.

3. THE WORLD'S BEST REGION FOR SAUVIGNON BLANC: LOIRE VALLEY, FRANCE

Villages such as Sancerre and Pouilly-Fumé in northern France's Loire Valley make a uniquely stylish midweight white wine from all Sauvignon Blanc grapes. These

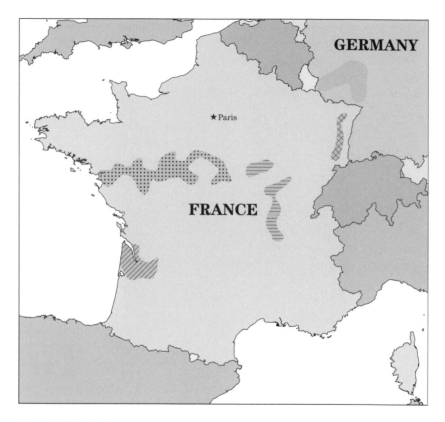

French Wine Regions

 Loire Valley region

 Bordeaux region

 Burgundy region

 Alsace region

German Wine Regions

bracingly tart wines are very dry and make exceptionally flexible food partners; their understatement and finesse are part of their appeal.

RUNNER-UP: NEW ZEALAND. New Zealand's unusual climate is well-suited to Sauvignon Blanc. These wines take their cues from the Loire Valley wines mentioned above but display more vivid aromatics and stronger flavor.

4. THE WORLD'S BEST REGION FOR RIESLING: GERMANY

Riesling is a great grape that is widely misunderstood. Though many Americans regard this variety as a wine for novices, it has an inherent nobility that stands out, even among the world's finest grapes. Riesling produces an unusually diverse range of styles, from dry to sweet and from flinty to peachy. Other areas of the world may come close, but none do Riesling better than its native Germany.

RUNNER-UP: ALSACE, FRANCE. The French approach to Riesling is more consistently dry, yielding stronger and fuller-bodied wines than those from Germany. Stylish and food-friendly, Alsace Rieslings rank among the world's most expressive white wines.

MARNIE'S CORNER

In almost every case, the areas highlighted here are the native regions of these grape varieties. That is hardly coincidental. Classic regions and their distinctive wines are the source for our modern ideas of what constitutes a fine wine. Over centuries, vintners in these regions have refined their grapes and techniques in pursuit of excellence at a time when others were still choosing quantity over quality. Today, any winemaker using these grapes has been inspired, to a certain degree, by the original French or German "icons."

CHAPTER
FOUR

Wine and Food Pairing

FOR MOST WINE DRINKERS, THE BURNING QUESTIONS AREN'T ABOUT GRAPES OR WINEMAKING, AGING POTENTIAL OR LABELING LAW. WHAT MOST OF US WANT TO know is what to drink with what. With any other beverage, the answer would be simple: Drink what you like! And to a large degree, the same holds true with wine. But there's a catch. Wine has an unusually mercurial nature when it comes to pairing: It changes personality in the presence of food.

Everything we put in our mouths alters how we perceive the next taste, and this phenomenon occurs more dramatically with wine than with other beverages. It may sound strange, but wines you love to drink alone may fall flat when served with certain dishes. The reverse is also true: Wines you dislike on first sip may become gastronomic delights in the right food context. No wonder we all want pairing advice from those in the know.

Pairing is part science, part art; framing ideas, such as pairing wines and foods of similar weight and intensity, and erring on the side of lighter wines are a great place to start. Understanding more about sensory patterns and how we taste helps, too. Most people already have excellent instincts for pairing and just need enough reinforcement to trust them. Sommeliers and wine professionals know a thing or two about wine and food chemistry that can help unlock a world of new pairing possibilities.

When the right wine meets the right dish, time can slow and even stop for a moment. Pairings like these make the lifetime highlights reel. It's well worth experimenting to find those special wine–food connections and learning strategies for avoiding unpleasant ones.

HOW TO GET STARTED PAIRING WINE AND FOOD

EVAN GOLDSTEIN
Master Sommelier

W HEN IT'S TIME to pick a wine for dinner, people often don't know where to begin. Conflicting messages make it hard to know which expert to listen to. Some say there are prescriptive rules to follow; others insist folks should just drink their favorite wine regardless of what's for dinner. In my experience, the truth falls somewhere between the two extremes.

We can honor and appreciate the classic pairings, refined over time, without giving up the right to try new things that break the rules. Based on sound sensory foundations, traditional matches are tried and true; they can help narrow a crowded field to improve the odds of finding synergy. Yet, everyone's tastes in food and wine are different. Classic combinations, such as Champagne and caviar, may be largely valid, but no amount of color-coding or region-matching can define perfect wine partners for every recipe for every palate. Without leeway for creativity, pairing wine and food can become overly academic and devoid of epicurean fun.

A solid approach is to work within the safety of a few established principles but to leave room for exploration. This tactic works best when we think about the big picture. For example, think about wine in terms of its building-

EVAN GOLDSTEIN is a master sommelier and one of the nation's most recognized wine professionals. He is the author of the critically acclaimed *Perfect Pairings: A Master Sommelier's Practical Advice for Partnering Wine with Food*. Goldstein's food and wine career began at age 19, and in 1987 he became the youngest candidate to pass the prestigious Master Sommelier examination. Since 1990, he has created wine and service education programs with some of the world's top wine companies. In addition, as a former two-term chairman and founding board member, he continues to train and examine candidates for the Court of Master Sommeliers.

block characteristics—such as acidity, oak, tannin, sugar, and alcohol—rather than worrying about specific aromatics, like citrus, green herbs, raspberries, or mushrooms. Orient to the food in the same way, considering the impact of preparation and seasoning on overall flavor, not just whether the central protein is fish or fowl, meat or vegetable. Sommeliers tend to work from a checklist of priorities rather than a database of Platonic pairing ideals. At the end of the day, flavor and style are more important than grape and region. If it tastes good, it is good, so relax and have some fun with it!

- **PAIRING WINE AND FOOD IS LIKE BALLROOM DANCING: SOMEONE HAS TO LEAD.**
  You can't have two stars of the show—one will have to take a backseat. Most of the time, we put the food first. After all, someone worked hard to make the dinner, and we can always open another bottle of the same wine. Wine is supposed to be the refreshment more than the main event, the quenching counterpoint between bites. Unless the meal is being planned around a special bottle, we generally let the food take the leading role. And remember that you can always adjust the food slightly (adding salt and pepper, for example), but not the wine (tannin or acid levels are fixed).

- **THINK ABOUT THE MENU OR OCCASION; THE MORE VARIED THE FOODS, THE LESS "SPECIFIC" THE WINE NEEDS TO BE.**
  How many dishes will be served? Will one wine accompany all courses? If so, chances are the best choices will be food friendly and midweight, not stylistically extreme. The most flexible wines, those with the best chance of pairing well across the board, tend to fall in the middle of the style spectrum. If only one wine must cover everything from salad to steak, a lighter red will work better than a heavy one and a richer white will be more versatile than a delicate one.

- **IF THE WINE CHOICE WILL BE DRIVEN BY A SINGLE DISH, ASK YOURSELF SOME QUESTIONS. FIRST, WHAT ARE THE INGREDIENTS?**
  In any given recipe, several flavors may compete for attention. The simplest dishes are those centered on a single ingredient, such as oysters on the half shell or fresh

mozzarella. With this type of purity in a dish, the lead flavor's singularity should drive the wine choice. Tuna is not eggplant, eggplant is not lamb—if a dish is tightly ingredient-focused, we can take our wine cues from there without worrying much about the other questions.

- **NEXT, CONSIDER HOW THE DISH WILL BE PREPARED.**
  We often think of pairing in terms of proteins alone, such as Chardonnay with chicken or Pinot Noir with pork, but this habit can lead us astray. For example, the flavor impact of poaching is different from that of grilling. Although carpaccio is a beef dish, it probably cannot handle the big Cabernet we'd pair with seared sirloin steak. Think of preparations on a scale of impact, or degree of influence on overall flavor. Low-impact preparations start with serving items raw but also include steaming, poaching, and boiling. For these dishes, lighter wines can enhance without dominating. Medium-impact preparations include those that alter flavor, but not excessively, such as sautéing, deep frying, baking, and stir-frying. These methods can handle more flavor intensity and complexity in a wine partner, which will act just like an accenting sauce on the side. High-impact methods are those that leave a prominent flavor fingerprint on the food, such as grilling or smoking, especially with flavorful woods or charcoal. These amped-up flavors are better served with wines that are correspondingly bold and intense.

- **FINALLY, CONSIDER HOW THE DISH IS SEASONED. IS A SAUCE OR SPICE THE DOMINANT FLAVOR? IF SO, MATCH TO THE SEASONING, NOT TO THE PROTEIN.**
  Seasoning takes myriad forms, from marinades and spice rubs to sauces and glazes. If seasoning is a major factor in a recipe's flavor, it should also be the driving force behind wine pairing decisions. Although there are no limits on what might taste good, under these circumstances, traditional pairing patterns tend to favor like with like. For example, citrusy ceviche may be paired with a tart and tangy Sauvignon Blanc, whereas a creamy garlic aioli might call for a richer Chardonnay. A Provençal spice rub could be matched with a peppery Rhône red, or a port-wine reduction might favor a raisiny Zinfandel. Regardless of whether you follow the beaten track or blaze a new

trail, there's no question that the best pairings are those that orient to the strongest flavors on the plate, not just to the main ingredient.

MARNIE'S CORNER

Wine's weight and intensity are important factors in choosing what to pair with what, but few people are sure what they're looking for. Wine isn't rocket science, and our familiarity with food can help us grasp complex wine concepts. People instinctively think of salads as being lighter than soups and seafood as lighter than red meat. This isn't driven by calories or portion size as much as by fat content and flavor impact (aka *weight* and *intensity*). Therefore, oily avocado feels heavier than asparagus, and flavor-dense venison seems stronger than veal. Richness also boosts perceived intensity, so the fattiest foods will seem bolder in flavor, too—for example, blue cheese. Wines work more or less the same way. Where fats feel rich and boost flavor in food, alcohol plays a similiar role in wine. The wines with the highest alcohol are richest in texture and will often be the most concentrated in flavor.

HOW TO PAIR MORE GRACEFULLY BY CHOOSING LIGHT-BODIED WINES

TERRY THEISE
Wine Importer

MARNIE WANTS ME to share some pithy advice on why light-bodied wines, so often neglected, are worth exploring. Well, that's pretty simple, really. (1) Sheer firepower doesn't help wine play well with food partners, but vibrancy and grace do. (2) Wines on the lighter, brighter side are often—in a delicious twist of purest irony—more fairly priced than their muscle-bound peers. There is clarity, an almost crystalline purity, to fine light-bodied wines. This transparency of flavor allows you to consider its structure and enjoy its nuances, teaching you that nuance and structure are important. Train your palate this way and you'll be a better taster, period, as well as a more informed voter and a finer human being.

- **BIGGER IS NOT BETTER. BETTER IS BETTER.**

  Don't get me wrong. There's a time for heavy things. It's cold outside, you're starved or bored or depressed or whatever, and that lamb shank you've been wet-roasting for six hours is your best friend. It's just not every goddamn day.

TERRY THEISE is an influential wine importer based in Silver Spring, Maryland, specializing in fine estate wines from Germany, Austria, and the Champagne region. Twice nominated as the James Beard Foundation's Outstanding Wine and Spirits Professional, he was also recognized in 2005 as Importer of the Year by *Food & Wine* magazine. He has introduced American sommeliers and wine drinkers to the forgotten pleasures of light-bodied wine styles. His *Terry Theise Estates Collection* catalogs are sought out as much for his profound essays and biting humor as for his remarkable wines.

There's confusion over this issue, so I don't hesitate to repeat myself when it comes to first principles. It isn't the *extent* of the flavor that tells, but its quality. We've all had big wines that were dull and crude, and we've all had relatively little wines that simply tasted lovely. Yet in our skewered age, we have been convinced that forceful alcohol and a gratuitous wash of oaky pancake makeup are the hallmarks of fine wine.

- **DON'T BELIEVE THE HYPE.**
Scores and social yardsticks are pushing wine drinkers toward density and concentration, toward flavor that can break bricks with its head! We have become so besotted by our demand for impact that we risk forgetting how to discern beauty. Beauty is more important than impact. Harmony is more important than intensity.

- **PRICE IS A BETTER REFLECTION OF SUPPLY AND DEMAND THAN QUALITY.**
Fashion exerts a kind of mass hypnosis. Currently, the market is crawling like lemmings toward wines of shock and awe. Someday, I suspect we'll look back on this current obsession with intensity as we do other past follies of fashion. We'll be eyeing the dusty-bottled equivalents of wide lapels and bell-bottoms in the cellar, asking, "What was I thinking?" But, not too soon, I hope. I'd hate to see Napa Cabernet pricing applied to German Rieslings just yet.

- **THE STRONGER THE WINE, THE MORE UNWIELDY IT IS WITH FOOD.**
Monsters with 14 percent alcohol and higher are clunky with most appetizers and overwhelm all but the boldest main courses. Plus, they actually depress both the palate and the entire somatic system. Who wants the feeling of having had enough wine before the second course is served?

Wines of this warrior class manhandle the palate into submission and squash the appetite like a bug. They make it difficult to experience a true wine–food synergy unless you're spit-roasting a mastodon—in which case, bring on the Old Vine Zin! And, in a deeper sense, such powerhouse wines confuse us about the higher pleasures of drinking wine. They're like watching television; they do all the work for you, leaving you prone and passive. That might be appropriate for a lap dance, but not for a dance.

- **THE LIGHTER THE WINE, THE MORE FLEXIBLE IT IS WITH FOOD.**
Light-bodied wines stimulate appetite and create a lovely sense of anticipation. Such wines can enhance even the richest foods, shining a spotlight that heightens their flavor. Lighter styles are delicate, yes. But like slender gymnasts, their grace is not weakness. Bear in mind, the rubric of "light" wine can (and does) include wines with *tons* of flavor, often with tremendous range.

    Wine's role, indeed the role of any beverage at the table, is to refresh the senses, to provide counterpoint for savory food. From Champagne to Riesling, from Vinho Verde to Pinot Noir, light-bodied wines can do so in almost any gastronomic circumstance.

    Ready to try lighter wines? Here are some pointers for finding them:

1. **CHECK THE FINE PRINT FOR LOW ALCOHOL CONTENT.** Light-bodied wines will be at or below 13 percent. Alcohol content correlates with wine's perceived weight, or "body."
2. **EMBRACE A WHITER SHADE OF PALE.** Light-bodied styles are most often white wines, such as Riesling and Albariño, and sparkling wines, such as Champagne and Prosecco. Reds are less common, like red Burgundy and Rioja, and often more translucent than opaque.
3. **LOOK TO THE NORTH TO SEE THE LIGHTEST-BODIED WINES.** The coolest climates produce the most light-bodied wines, namely Germany, Austria, northern France, and northern Italy.
4. **"CHILL OUT" NEAR THE OCEAN.** Cool coastal regions may also favor the lighter side, from Portuguese Vinho Verde to Tasmanian sparklers.

MARNIE'S CORNER

For years, I was sommelier for a restaurant with an all-seafood menu. It didn't take long for me to shed my "bigger is better" prejudices. I no longer judge a wine by its strength or by the color of its (grape's) skin. Strangely, novices and experts alike tend to love whites and light-bodied wines, although those with a little wine experience may shy away. There is a pernicious preconception that wines low in alcohol or high in sugar cannot possibly be good. These ideas are deeply misguided and corrosive, leading generations of wine drinkers to feel that they must unlearn their love for a style of wine that tastes naturally delicious. But luckily for open-minded beginners like you, that means the whole world isn't fighting over these light-bodied wines. All the more for us. Hooray!

HOW TO FIND DELICIOUS COMBINATIONS BY "MATCHING" COLORS

FRED DEXHEIMER
Master Sommelier

THE UNDERLYING PRINCIPLES of successful wine and food pairing are simple. Take color, for example. Did you know that the same instincts we rely on for coordinating our clothes can help us choose flattering wines to serve with dinner? Restaurant guests might not realize what the sommelier is up to, but often we're matching wines to food by color.

It may sound odd, but we can taste color in food and wine. Broccoli tastes more like similarly colored green beans than like vegetables of other colors, such as carrots. Color and flavor may be perceived by different senses, but in many cases they correspond to the same compounds. The pigmented skins of red grapes impart flavor; the effect of oxidation in wine is perceived as both a browning of color and a caramelization of flavor.

I first started using food color as a wine guide when working with seafood. The darker the sauce and the darker the flesh of the fish, the more likely the dish could handle a red wine partner. Sommeliers often look to sauces for color cues. With pastas, white wines are matched with cream sauces, red wines with tomato sauces. For meats, darker reds are matched with the darkest reduction sauces,

FRED DEXHEIMER is an award-winning master sommelier and serves as the national wine and beverage director for the famed BLT Restaurant Group. He mentors a burgeoning team of talented sommeliers who articulate his vision throughout acclaimed Chef Laurent Tourondel's growing family of restaurants. Dexheimer is also involved with United Sommeliers, a movement led by wine professionals dedicated to creating a community of passionate, experienced sommeliers countrywide. An avid runner, he fuels his passion for fitness by participating in New York City charity races.

paler reds with simple au jus, or pan juices. Sometimes, the color of the protein provides inspiration. Here are some color-swatching thoughts to bear in mind the next time you're choosing wine to pair with a dish.

- **GREEN FOOD? THINK PALE WHITE WINES WITH A "GREEN" CHARACTER.**
  The whitest white wines often show a faint glint of green color and a whiff of "green" aromatics. From Sauvignon Blanc to Grüner Veltliner, and from Riesling to Albariño, these wines are terrific choices for leafy green salads and green vegetables. They're also delicious with fresh green herbs, such as basil, cilantro, mint, and parsley, and pair particularly pleasantly with sauces or preparations with a base of extra virgin olive oil. Lime, lemon, and green apple are green-tasting accents, too.

- **YELLOW FOOD? THINK YELLOW-WHITE WINES WITH A "GOLDEN" CHARACTER.**
  Some white wine styles are less water-white than honey-gold, notably older wines or full-bodied styles that are given oak treatment. The color shift is primarily a result of oxidation (just as sliced pears will turn first yellow then brown if exposed to air), but it may also be boosted by the fire-toasted surfaces of oak barrels. With wines, gold usually tastes richer than green; think of the taste differences between golden delicious versus granny smith apples. The quintessential golden wine is Chardonnay, whose color deepens with oak influence, but such styles as Viognier and Pinot Gris can flirt with yellow tones as well. These are perfect choices for a yellow sauce made with butter, cream, or eggs, and they naturally flatter yellow foods such as corn, mango, and pineapple. Golden wines complement golden seasonings, like saffron, as well as the golden "browning" of food during cooking.

- **PINK FOOD? THINK ROSÉ WINES WITH A "PINK" FLAVOR.**
  Rosé wines pair well with almost everything, particularly with foods that have a pinkish hue. Cured meats are a natural, especially prosciutto, soppresatta, ham, and even hot dogs. Seafood such as salmon, tuna, shrimp, crab, and lobster, which usually can't quite handle red wine, will often shine with rosé. Also try them when a touch of

FOOD AND WINE PAIRING BY COLOR

TYPE OF FOOD		TYPE OF WINE
	Green: Lettuce, broccoli, green beans, lemons/limes	Sauvignon Blanc Riesling Grüner Veltliner Albariño
	Yellow: Corn, pineapple, butter/cream, mango	Chardonnay Viognier Pinot Gris
	Pink: Ham, shrimp, lobster, hot dogs	Rosé

tomato adds a blush of color and flavor to pasta or when beets supply mauvy goodness to a salad.

- **ORANGE-RED OR BROWN-RED FOOD? THINK PALER RED WINES.**
  Among red wines, those made from thinner-skinned grapes, such as Pinot Noir and Grenache, will always look most translucent. These wines tend to oxidize quickly,

TYPE OF FOOD		TYPE OF WINE
	Orange-Red/Brown-Red: Mushrooms, chicken, tomatoes	Pinot Noir Grenache Sangiovese (Chianti)
	Purple-Red/Blackened: Beef, lamb, BBQ foods	Cabernet Sauvignon Shiraz/Syrah Merlot Malbec
	Rainbow: Ice cream, strawberries, lemon meringue pie	Asti (white) Icewine, late harvest (yellow) Sauternes, Tokaji Aszú (gold) Brachetto (pink) Port (purple) Pedro Ximenez (brown)

losing their pinkish youth to a brick-red tinge with a little barrel or bottle age. They naturally suit sauces based on stewed tomatoes or red wine, natural broths, or gravies. As these wines mature and their color turns rusty, they become better suited for wild mushrooms, as well as Madeira and Marsala sauces. Very flexible with proteins, these wines can flatter slow-cooked poultry and light meats and simply prepared dark meats, as well as dark-flesh steak fish (cooked, not raw).

- **PURPLE-RED OR BLACKENED FOOD? THINK DARKER RED WINES.**
  Thick-skinned grapes yield the deepest, darkest wines, including Cabernet Sauvignon, Shiraz, and Malbec. Such wines are best paired with the darkest red meats, such as beef, lamb, and venison, and the darkest sauces, like veal stock reductions and barbeque. The deepening and darkening of flavor imparted by grilling can boost paler foods into this realm as well.

- **A SIMILAR "RAINBOW" APPROACH IS APPLIED EVEN MORE SUCCESSFULLY TO SWEET DESSERT WINES.**
  Pair the palest sweet wines, such as Asti and Icewine, with ice cream or lemon meringue pie. Try such golden nectars as Sauternes and Tokaji Aszu with golden custards (crème brûlée) and orchard fruit desserts (peach and other cobblers). Frothy fuschia Brachetto is ideal with pink strawberries, and mahogany sherries like Pedro Ximenez flatter dark brown delights like gingersnaps and pecan pie. When it comes to the darkest chocolate, there's nothing better than an inky glass of Port.

MARNIE'S CORNER

Color compounds are good for us, providing a rich source of antioxidants. They're also hard for plants to produce since their construction requires much energy from the sun. In general, the deepest, darkest grape colors correspond to the warmest, sunniest climates. Green, yellow, and white fruits and berries are most often found in the coolest regions. Green grapes and white wines are specialties of the coolest wine zones. Purple, red, and blue pigments need more sunshine to develop, so we associate dark grapes and red wines with warmer regions.

HOW TO UNDERSTAND
UMAMI—THE FAMOUS
"FIFTH TASTE"

DOUG FROST
Master of Wine & Master Sommelier

THOUGH IT WAS discovered nearly a century ago, the taste sensation known as *umami* still provokes considerable disagreement, at least outside the scientific community.

Some in the culinary world believe that umami is responsible whenever anything tastes good, whereas recalcitrants try to deny its existence entirely. But the truth about umami lies somewhere in between. It definitely exists, but it is only one of many factors that create flavor in, and boost enjoyment from, foods and wines.

One of the most heated points of contention is umami's role in food and wine pairings. As for many gastronomic questions, the answers are highly subjective. To make matters worse, umami is a slippery fish; easily confused with other sensations, it is extremely challenging to study. It's worth reviewing what we know and what we don't know about this once mysterious "fifth taste."

Kansas City author **DOUG FROST** is one of only three people in the world to have achieved the remarkable distinctions of master sommelier and master of wine. He has written three books: *Uncorking Wine* (1996), *On Wine* (2001), and *Far from Ordinary Spanish Wine Buying Guide* (2005), now in its second edition. Frost is the wine and spirits consultant for United Airlines and writes for many national publications. He spends his spare time listening to his massive punk rock and weird music collection.

- **UMAMI IS A PLEASANT TASTE SENSATION.**
  Umami is one of at least five flavor sensations—along with sweetness, saltiness, bitterness, and acidity—that are truly "tasted" with the receptors on the tongue and

in the mouth. Tastes are designed to send a message to our bodies about the food we're eating. For example, because sugar is a source of energy, sweetness is generally perceived as a positive attribute. Bitterness, on the other hand, warns of potentially harmful compounds in food and is more typically an unpleasant sensation. Umami is associated with proteins and other nutritious components, and therefore it is received as a pleasant, even rich, sensation. It has been variously called "the flavor of protein," "the flavor of chicken soup," or "the flavor of deliciousness." The umami flavor has not been a traditional focus when Westerners speak about food and flavor. As a result, some speak of umami as a flavor amplifier, more than as a flavor in its own right. But, like the other main flavors, umami has distinct receptor sites in the human mouth and is a distinct flavor.

- **UMAMI IS NATURALLY PRESENT IN MANY FLAVORFUL FOODS.**
Identified and named in 1911 in Japan, umami is made up of organic compounds: the amino acids known as glutamates and certain nucleotides. Organic compounds that trigger umami sensation are found naturally in all sorts of foods. They have also been a prominent component of "flavored" foods for half a century, the best known being monosodium glutamate, or MSG.

  Umami-rich foods include everything from fresh produce to aged cheeses. Shellfish, seaweed, and mushrooms are strong sources of umami as well. Meats score high in umami, especially when slow cooked, as in stews or soups. In addition, when two different umami components are combined, the effect is amplified. Many classic combinations capitalize on this fact, such as the veal and onion stock that serves as the base of many French sauces, or the seaweed and dried-fish broth that is central to Japanese cuisine. Some scientists believe that aged wines contain significant umami components, but this theory remains unproven.

- **THERE IS MUCH DEBATE ABOUT UMAMI'S IMPACT ON OTHER FLAVORS.**
Since sensation is individual and varied in each of us, it's not surprising there is so little consensus. There are no universal food or drink experiences, and by extension there are no universal experiences of food and drink in combination. You may like

Brussels sprouts; I may find them annoying. I might enjoy liver and onions; you might be repulsed. It is difficult to study umami's effect on other flavors, at least in terms of stating universal principles.

- **TO DATE, MOST OBSERVABLE PATTERNS IN UMAMI INTERACTIONS WITH WINE INVOLVE ITS EFFECT ON THE TANNIC BITTERNESS OF RED WINE.**
Umami seems to amplify the astringent component in red wines, known as tannin. But as with many sensory experiences, the negative opinion is not shared by everyone. Although many find that umami and tannin together leave a metallic taste, some find the combination less unpleasant. For example, pairing oysters and tannic red wine seems intuitively wrong. The high umami content of oysters may be the culprit, emphasizing tannic bitterness. But some people do not consider the two to be a poor match.

Conversely, aged and well-cooked meats have plenty of umami, but no one seems to complain about the metallic effect of cooked meats on red wines. Experiments suggest that other elements, such as fats, proteins, and salt, may neutralize the effect somewhat, providing a counterbalance to the red wine's tannins. Most people find red wines a happy match with meat dishes.

- **THE KEY TO POSITIVE COMBINATIONS IS BALANCE—OF THE LEVELS OF UMAMI AND OTHER TASTE COMPONENTS—IN BOTH THE FOOD AND THE WINE.**
Discussions about pairing with umami can make your head spin. But if there is one simplifying rule, it may be this: If both the food and the wine are balanced among the primary flavors of salty, sweet, bitter, sour, and umami, they are likely to go well with just about any other well-balanced food or wine. Chefs know that incorporating a touch of each flavor makes a dish more satisfying. It also helps to flatter the flavors of the wine being served.

And if all this makes you long for beer and chips, fret not. The business of food and wine matching is complicated only if you try to explain it. If you're simply trying to enjoy it, then drink and eat whatever you damn well please.

MARNIE'S CORNER

The term *umami* derives from the Japanese words *umai* ("deliciousness") and *mi* ("essence"). For Americans this taste sensation may be less recognizable than salt or sweet, but it is all around us nonetheless. From our first experience with our mothers' milk, which is loaded with umami, we are attuned to this rich protein taste. Many of the sauces and seasonings we use to improve food flavor are umami rich, from ketchup to soy sauce, dashi to Worcestershire sauce.

HOW TO PAIR WINE WITH CHALLENGING VEGETABLES

NATALIE MACLEAN
Wine Author

W HEN IT COMES to pairing wine and food, there's good news and bad news. First the good news: Wine is naturally food friendly, so most food and wine combinations taste better together than apart. Yay! The bad news: A few food categories do throw wine drinkers a curveball. Darn.

Vegetables top the list of wine-pairing problem children. Even nondrinkers seem to have heard that artichokes and asparagus shouldn't be paired with wine, and some experts have given up on broad categories, such as salads and bitter greens. Yet more of us are eating the leafy green stuff these days and still want to enjoy a glass of vino. Luckily, there's hope! Although some vegetables do pose a challenge, they simply require a little more thought to find a delicious match.

Let traditionalists sputter about which veggie doesn't go with what. Not me. I am a determined hedonist. Life is simply too short *not* to drink wine with everything, so I've never been one to admit defeat. In my experience, tasty wine pairings exist for every plant, from artichokes to eggplants. The same basic principles apply to pairing any

NATALIE MACLEAN is the author of the best-seller *Red, White, and Drunk All Over: A Wine-Soaked Journey from Grape to Glass,* the winner in the wine book category at the Gourmand World Cookbook Awards. She was named the World's Best Drink Writer at the World Food Media Awards in Australia and has won four James Beard journalism awards, including the MFK Distinguished Writing Award. Her free wine e-newsletter containing wine picks, food matches, cellar advice, articles, and humor is available on her Web site.

wine with any food: Think light with light, rich with rich, and try to harmonize flavors overall. Here are some quick tips for veggie-friendly wines.

- **THE WHITE STUFF IS THE RIGHT STUFF FOR VEGETABLES.**
White wines, whether they're dry or lightly sweet, almost always match more pleasantly with salads and vegetarian cuisine than reds do. When the veggies are served uncooked, look to fresh, young, unoaked whites, such as Pinot Grigio. Sauvignon Blanc—loaded with "green" herbal flavors—complements greens of all kinds, from leafy lettuce to herb sauces. White wine styles that are richer and less tart, including Chardonnay, are better choices for sweet or starchy vegetables, like corn, squash, and carrots. Dishes enriched with oil or butter can handle the full-bodied whites, whereas those with smoky or nutty flavors will go best with oaky wines.

- **AVOID THE WRONG KINDS OF WINES, ESPECIALLY THOSE POPULAR "BIG REDS."**
Lusty red wines—Cabernet Sauvignon and Syrah, to name but two—pair brilliantly with protein-rich meats but turn ugly when served with protein-free veggies. Not only do they overwhelm flavor-wise, they also seem extra harsh and tannic. Even midweight reds tend to clash with vegan dishes if they are dry, mature, and complex, such as French Bordeaux or Italian Brunello.

    If you're a diehard red wine fan and a vegetarian, don't despair. First, you can boost the flavor intensity of almost any recipe by grilling, roasting, or slow-cooking or by adding red-wine-friendly ingredients, such as mushrooms or cheese. Then ease back on the vinous throttle and choose young, soft reds, perhaps Pinot Noir or Beaujolais.

- **BE CAREFUL, NOT FEARFUL, WITH ARTICHOKES AND ASPARAGUS.**
Artichokes are loaded with cyanin, a com-pound that can create a weird alternate uni-verse of wine flavor since it makes everything taste oddly saccharine-sweet. Searingly dry and acidic whites—such as Italian Verdicchio and Vernaccia—can hold their own against it.

Most often this vegetable is an accent, not the main event, and therefore is not overly problematic. Slow-cooking also breaks down cyanin, especially if wine or lemon is added.

Asparagus, with far less cyanin, often gets lumped in with the artichoke. However, it really doesn't deserve its reputation as a wine killer. Asparagus spears may not flatter monster red wines or butter-bomb Chardonnays, but they can be delightful with whites whose aromatics show similar herbal green aromas, such as Sauvignon Blanc from New Zealand and Austrian Grüner Veltliner.

- **WHEN VINEGAR TAKES THE LEAD (THINK SALADS AND PICKLES), CHOOSE A WINE WITH VIBRANT ACIDITY.**
  With these dishes, it's more often the volatile vinegar than the vegetable flavors that throw the wine for an ugly loop. Our senses simply cannot handle more than one source of similar sensation simultaneously. Strongly acidic components like vinegar effectively block wine's weaker acidity, which can flatten the wine's flavor and leave it seeming less than refreshing. If toning down the vinegar isn't an option, look to the wines with taut acidity, including sparkling wine, Muscadet, and dry Riesling.

- **GOT A VEGGIE I DIDN'T COVER? PAIR YOUR WINE ONLINE.**
  After receiving countless questions about pairing wine with veggies and other challenging foods, I created an interactive food-and-wine matcher on my Web site. The matching tool is updated regularly and pairs wines with any dish: meat, pasta, seafood, vegetarian, pizza, eggs, cheese, and even dessert, including JELL O and fudge (for those who like to layer their vices). Got a dish or a wine to stump me? Just e-mail me via my Web site and I'll suggest a match for you.

MARNIE'S CORNER

Wine is a natural counterpoint to rich, salty, and starchy foods; when we picture a meal with wine, we're more likely to envision meat, cheese, and bread than string beans, beets, and broccoli. Vegetarian cuisine can be delightful with wine, but it does require a few adjustments. As a general rule of thumb, choose lighter-bodied wines when making a meatless and dairy-free version of any recipe. Body can be guesstimated from the wine's alcohol content, which will always appear on the label. Remember, the lower the alcohol, the lighter the wine.

HOW TO CHOOSE WINES FOR FOODS WITH A SPICY KICK

GUY STOUT
Master Sommelier

S PICY FOOD HAS a prickly relationship with wine. Some people are convinced that wine can't take the heat, and so they opt for beer or cocktails instead. It's true that spicy heat poses more challenges for wine than for other drinks. But take it from me—wine can be a terrific partner for hot dishes. The key is to learn how wine interacts with spicy foods on the sensory level. Once you have a grip on how it works, picking wine for your favorite hot stuff becomes much easier.

When we say *spicy food*, we don't just mean extra-seasoned. "Spicy" means seasoned with specific spices that cause a distinctive "hot" sensation on contact. Technically speaking, these spices activate chemesthesis in skin and palate tissues; in plain English, they *burn*—sometimes painfully so.

Many chemical compounds in food cause this spicy heat effect, like gingerol in ginger and piperine in black pepper. But chili peppers take the cake for pure heat, thanks to capsaicin, the compound responsible for everything from the mild warmth of pepperoncinis to the blast-furnace firepower of habañeros.

GUY STOUT is a master sommelier and corporate director of beverage education for Glazer's, a fine wine and spirits distributor in twelve states. He is active in the wine community and serves on the board of directors of the Society of Wine Educators and the Texas Sommelier Association. Stout has been featured as a wine expert on the PBS cooking series *Cucina Amore*, with Damian Mandola and Johnny Carrabba, founders of the Carrabba's restaurant chain. He is also an owner of Stout Vineyards, in the Texas Hill Country American Viticultural Area (AVA), where he produces Syrah grapes for local wineries.

- **SPICINESS IS A PHYSICAL SENSATION OF BURNING OR HEAT; IT'S NOT A TASTE OR SMELL.**
  We call spicy foods "hot" because they literally feel hot when we come into contact with them. Thermo-sensitive nerves are stimulated and chili peppers and ginger feel warm, just as mint and eucalyptus feel cool. This sensation doesn't wipe away with a napkin or rinse off with water. Once we encounter a compound like capsaicin, we're stuck with the "chemical burn" until it fades on its own. As Chef Robert Del Grande of Houston's Café Annie says, "Once the heat hits, the only relief is to distract yourself."

- **THE BURN OF HOT SPICES AND SAUCES IS MILDLY PAINFUL BUT STIMULATES THE SENSES.**
  Eating spicy food is like riding a roller coaster—the adrenaline rush reminds you that you're alive. If spicy foods were only a source of pain, we'd never eat them. The truth is that eating the hot stuff is a huge turn-on, a shock to the system similar to jumping into a cold lake on a baking hot day. Although burning pain seems like something to avoid, it can also be a gateway to pleasure by heightening the senses. Food is not naturally spicy; we apply hot sauces, spices, or seasonings to food. If we didn't like the heat, we would get the spicy stuff out of the kitchen.

- **ALCOHOL FANS THE FLAMES OF SPICY HEAT. THE STRONGER THE DRINK, THE MORE IT WILL BURN.**
  We expect a cold drink to relieve spicy heat, but if the beverage is alcoholic, we get the opposite result. Alcohol boosts the fiery sensation on the palate rather than rinsing it away. The higher the alcohol content, the more vivid the effect will be (similar to pouring gas on a barbeque). This helps explain why the very hottest foods, such as Mexican or Indian cuisines, are paired more with low-alcohol beer than with high-alcohol wine or martinis.

- **THE WINES THAT BURN THE MOST WITH HOT FOODS ARE DRY, FULL-BODIED REDS.**
  The higher a wine's alcohol content, the more it will inflame the palate and intensify the burn of spicy heat. Alcohol is most volatile at the warmest temperatures, so the

effect is strongest when the wine is room temperature and weakest when the wine is chilled. Super-spicy food is rarely flattering with full-bodied red wines such as Cabernet Sauvignon or Malbec, particularly when these are served at 75°F (24°C) or above. The heat leaves the wine tasting too bitter and boozy, and the wine makes the food seem scorchingly hot.

- **LIGHT-BODIED WINES CAN TAME SPICY HEAT, ESPECIALLY IF THEY'RE A LITTLE SWEET AND SERVED COLD, LIKE SOME WHITES, ROSÉS, AND SPARKLERS.**
  Light white wines are less problematic with the hottest dishes. The lower the alcohol, the better. Sugar can also soothe your burning mouth after fiery foods, and many of the lightest-bodied white and pink wines aren't fully dry. Not only does cool wine feel better to the touch after a blast of spice, but a lower temperature slows evaporation and reduces the aggressive after-burn of alcohol. From delicate German Riesling to modest California White Zinfandel, the lightest, sweetest wines are often the most flattering partners for the spiciest foods.

MARNIE'S CORNER

The taste for spicy food isn't universal—it is individual, with a strong dose of cultural adaptation. Tolerance for heat varies widely from one person to another. Some people are genetically sensitive to spicy heat, finding it so painful that they avoid it entirely. Others crave the invigorating heart-pounding, sweat-inducing effect. Also, our bodies adapt to spiciness; the more hot stuff we eat, the more we develop a tolerance. It can take a lot more capsaicin for those raised in a "spicy food culture" to even notice heat. So whether you want to amplify or soften the sensations of spicy heat will largely be determined by personal preferences. If you love the full-body impact of fiery foods, choose stronger, drier wines. If you just want to flirt with the hot stuff and retreat to safety, you'll be better off with light, off-dry styles.

HOW TO PAIR WITH SWEET DESSERT WINES

DONALD ZIRALDO
Vintner & Wine Author

DESSERT WINES MAKE remarkable food partners, and not just with desserts. These jewels of the wine world are terrific with other dishes, too, from lamb shank to French toast. However, since so few fine wines are as delicious alone, people sometimes forget how truly amazing they can taste with food.

Throughout history, people have craved sweet wines. They aren't easy to make, and doing it well pushes the limits of both grape growing and winemaking to extremes. Ounce for ounce, dessert wines are unrivalled in the amount of effort, sacrifice, and patience required in their production. Exceptional dessert wines are something very special—the ultimate expression of grape and vineyard combined.

Standard winemaking involves converting the natural sugar in fresh grapes into alcohol through fermentation. Therefore, even though grapes are sweet, most wines are not. Their natural state is dry, the opposite of sweet. Dessert winemakers must somehow produce a wine that is both sweet and alcoholic. Dessert wine needs to have it all: enough alcohol to be stable, enough sugar to be fully sweet, enough acidity to taste balanced, and enough flavor to be objects of desire. Achieving all of these at once is a

Pioneer of Canada's estate winery movement, **DONALD ZIRALDO** is cofounder of the award-winning Inniskillin Wines, in the Niagara-on-the-Lake region. He has worked to bring Icewine and Canadian wines to the world. As founding chair of Ontario's Vintners Quality Alliance, Ziraldo's commitment to quality was a driving force behind the establishment of the ambitious Canadian wine regulatory system. His latest book, *Icewine: Extreme Winemaking*, explores the art and science of this painstaking pursuit of beauty in the glass. In addition to serving as chair of Ontario's Vineland Research and Innovation Center, he collects art deco objets and skis internationally.

tall order that often entails drastically reduced yields of wine per vineyard acre. As a result, even small bottles of top dessert wines can be pricey.

Different regions worldwide have found different ways to meet the rigorous requirements of dessert wine, each working within unique local circumstances. In warm regions, grapes may be partially sun dried, for example, as for Vin Santo; in cold regions, they may be allowed to hang on the vine into midwinter and freeze solid, as for Icewine. The techniques vary greatly in their impact on flavor, style, sweetness, and texture. Grouping dessert wines by such characteristics is the key to deciding how to proceed in partnering dessert wines with food.

- **SWEET WINE AND SWEET DESSERTS CAN SHINE TOGETHER, PROVIDED THAT THE DESSERT IS LESS SWEET THAN THE WINE.**
  Desserts are the most common matches for sweet dessert wines, and their synergy can be fantastic, as long as one overriding condition is met: The sweetness of the dessert must not exceed the level of sweetness in the wine.

- **SWEET WINE AND SAVORY FOODS CAN MAKE FOR AN UNEXPECTEDLY DELICIOUS COMBINATION.**
  When stepping outside the dessert course, sweet wines are typically most flattering with rich foods, such as cheeses and meats, as opposed to low-fat dishes, for example, salads and sushi. The fattier the food, the more it can handle the opulent texture of top dessert wines, including Icewine and Sauternes. Sweet accents or sauces used in cooking—fresh or dried fruit, honey, brown sugar, molasses, or port wine—provide some of the best opportunities for choosing to serve dessert wines rather than dry wines with dinner.

- **LATE-HARVEST WINES ARE MADE FROM "SUPER-RIPE" GRAPES THAT HAVE GROWN SWEETER AND MORE FLAVORFUL ON THE VINE.**
  The most common means for making dessert wine involves leaving fruit to hang longer than usual before picking. Doing so boosts sugar and flavor, but it has risks, too. Some fruit is lost to spoilage, and acidity may drop too fast. The most common

late-harvest wines are midweight and mildly sweet; most are not very concentrated in flavor. Among desserts, they pair better with subtle flavors, such as pound cake and ice cream. Those with lower sugar content make great partners for dinner courses on the sweeter side, like beef teriyaki and duck à l'orange.

- **FROZEN GRAPE WINES, OR ICEWINES, ARE COLD-CLIMATE SPECIALTIES THAT ARE DECADENTLY RICH AND SWEET, YET BEAUTIFULLY BALANCED.**
  Icewine takes the late-harvest concept as far as it can go. Vintners leave grapes hanging into the dead of winter and harvest them completely frozen. In daily freezing and thawing, shards of ice help break down cell walls, bringing more flavor compounds into the juice that remains. Natural Icewine production is possible only in the coldest vineyard regions, such as Canada, Germany, and Austria. The depth of flavor and tactile richness of the real thing, as well as the prodigious levels of sugar and balancing acidity, make these the world's most prized dessert wines. They grace rich, savory foods like triple cream cheeses and foie gras with panache. And since there is little danger of exceeding their sweetness, they are among the safest choice for a broad range of desserts, from flourless chocolate cake to mango mousse.

- **BOTRYTIS-AFFECTED DESSERT WINES CAPITALIZE ON A BENEV-OLENT FUNGUS THAT YIELDS HONEYED-TASTING WINES THAT RANGE IN SWEETNESS.**
  In cool but not cold regions, there is another method of amplifying sweetness and texture in dessert wine: to allow a fungus called *Botrytis cinerea* to infect late-harvest fruit. The fungus compromises the integrity of the grape skins, allowing internal moisture to evaporate more quickly than normal. This speeds the raisination process and concentrates sugar and flavor while allowing the acids to remain high. Also known as "noble rot," botrytis adds a distinctive honeyed aromatic to such classics as Sauternes, Beerenauslese, and Tokaji Aszú. After Icewine, this dessert wine style is the most versatile, and it is delightful with funkier cheeses like bleus and country pâtés. Among desserts, these wines tend to favor caramel and custard flavors as well as orchard fruits, such as those in apple tarte tatin or peach cobbler.

- **SUN-DRIED GRAPES GROW SWEETER AS THEY RAISINATE AND MAKE SWEET WINES WITH A "NUTTY" CHARACTER.**
One warm-climate method is to dry grapes in the sun after harvest to mimic late-harvest concentration. However, since the grapes are no longer "alive," they begin to oxidize and brown. Wines made this way—Vin Santo and sweet Sherry, for example—have a distinctive nutty flavor that tends to work best with foods that show a similar caramelized quality, as do French onion soup and fried foods. The sweetest are terrific with nut desserts like pecan pie, too.

- **FORTIFIED WINES HAVE EXTRA ALCOHOL ADDED TO BOOST BODY, OFTEN TO RETAIN GRAPE SWEETNESS.**
Another warm-climate approach to making sweet wine is to interrupt fermentation before all sugar is converted to alcohol. Port is made this way, by adding alcohol to kill off the yeasts midstream. In essence, these wines are really part wine, part grape juice, and part unrefined brandy. No wonder they're so "grapey" and alcoholic! The powerful red wine character of Port can overwhelm delicate foods and is best suited to potent flavors like chocolate and blue cheese.

MARNIE'S CORNER

The one thing to watch out for in pairing dessert wine with dessert is competing degrees of sweetness. If the dessert is sweeter than the wine, the wine may taste askew a little too sour or too thin. Our senses don't work like spreadsheets or bank accounts—one plus one doesn't equal two. Two sources of similar sensation—two sweet things, in this instance—will never make each other taste sweeter. Instead, they'll both seem less sweet together than they do apart. So keep the following in mind: The sweetest dessert wines are best for the sweetest desserts (such as crème brûlée), whereas those with less sweetness pair best with low-sugar desserts (like biscotti).

CHAPTER
FIVE

Wine in Restaurants

A RESTAURANT CAN BE THE BEST PLACE TO DRINK WINE. AFTER ALL, THE OFFERINGS HAVE BEEN SELECTED BY A PROFESSIONAL BUYER WITH THE ESTABLISHMENT'S menu in mind. Often someone is on hand to advise you on your decision. Some restaurants may even offer additional assets such as a selection of open wines by the glass to sample and plenty of stemware. Most important of all, wine in restaurants is served in its proper context.

Wine is the only beverage overtly designed to taste better with food than alone. So it's no surprise that restaurants provide outstanding wine experiences. Yet, many find ordering wine in restaurants to be more stressful than choosing wine in a retail shop. Evenings out carry more expectations than the average dinner at home, especially when we are celebrating special occasions, entertaining clients, or trying to make a good impression with a date. Fear of ordering the wrong thing or overspending can end up interfering with our enjoyment of the dining experience.

Yes, knowledge is power. But you needn't memorize French grapes or California vintages to drink well in restaurants, any more than you need to understand the workings of an engine to go for a nice drive. Rather than trying to memorize loads of wine data, ask the experts for a recommendation. Learning a little about how wine service works or how to tell whether to trust a restaurant's wine program will boost your confidence. A little savvy and an open mind are all most diners need to improve their wine experiences.

HOW TO GAUGE A
RESTAURANT'S WINE SAVVY

MARK OLDMAN
Wine Author

S O THE SERVER slides you the wine list and all eyes look your way. What should you do? Your first move should be to scope out the restaurant's attitude toward wine and, by extension, wine drinkers. This will help you determine whether you can feel safe in their hands or whether you should assume a defensive crouch to head off gustatory and financial ruin.

Wine service in restaurants varies widely. Even within a particular category—high-end steakhouses or casual burger joints—great variance exists in pricing policies, selling strategies, and levels of wine knowledge among staff. Some restaurants have soul-less wine programs, selling wine like widgets and squeezing every nickel out of it. In these eateries, you'll often be expected to pay up to five times the retail price. By contrast, if you find yourself in a restaurant that truly cares about its wine service, you'll likely find better wine for the dollar.

To help ascertain the type of restaurant you're in, consult the wine list for clues.

One of the country's leading wine educators, **MARK OLDMAN** is author of the best-selling *Oldman's Guide to Outsmarting Wine*, which won the Duboeuf "Best Wine Book of the Year" award. Passionate about helping wine enthusiasts jostle the jaded and slay the snooty, Oldman is the lead judge in the new PBS television series *The Winemakers* and regularly appears at the country's top gastronomic festivals. He writes for several leading lifestyle publications and contributes a wine column and chooses the wine picks for the hit magazine *Everyday with Rachael Ray*.

1. EXAMINE HOW THE WINE LIST LOOKS—COVER, PAPER, AND ALL.

A restaurant that cares about wine reflects that passion in the presentation of its wine list. Typos are a red flag. Be wary of grease spots and frayed covers. Yellowed or dog-eared pages suggest infrequent reprinting, a sign of neglect. Good wine lists often change every few weeks, so crisp, new pages are a welcome clue.

2. IS THE WINE LIST USER FRIENDLY?

Wine lists have traditionally been organized by either region or grape. But if you're a casual drinker, choosing wine this way can feel like a hapless game of Pin the Tail on the Donkey. Wine-savvy restaurants often incorporate flavor and style clues that reveal how the wines will taste. If you see headings such as "spicy," "smooth," and "fruity," you're likely in good hands.

3. HOW MUCH INFORMATION IS GIVEN FOR EACH WINE?

If wines are listed without basic information—such as vintages or, worse, producer names—consider pulling the vinous rip cord and opting for a frothy mug of beer. If, on the other hand, you find extra information—such as suggested food pairings or notations for sweet or cork-free wines—you're experiencing the fruits of a conscientious wine program.

NOT ENOUGH INFORMATION

HOUSE MERLOT *California* 22

STANDARD INFORMATION

MERLOT *Pepi*
2003 California 22

EXTRA INFORMATION

MERLOT *Pepi*
2003 California .... 22 [cork-free]

WHITE WINE FROM THE UNITED STATES

Pinot Gris

100	Chehalem, Willamette Valley, OR	2007	51
100	Adelsehim, Willamette Valley, OR	2006	37

Sauvignon Blanc and Fumé Blanc

103	Peter Michael L'Apres Midi, Sonoma County, CA	2006	121
104	Duckhorn, Napa Valley, CA	2007	68
105	Cakebread Cellars, Napa Valley, CA	2006	62
106	Provenance, Napa Valley, CA	2006	45
107	Grgich Hill Estate, Napa Valley, CA	2006	75

Chardonnay

110	Patz & Hall, Durell Ranch, Sonoma Coast, CA	2006	108
111	Jordan, Russian River Valley, Sonoma County, CA	2006	92
112	Matanzas Creek, Sonoma Valley, CA	2005	68
113	Rudd, Bacigalupi Vineyard, Napa Valley, CA	2005	168

Traditional Headings: *By Region/Grape*

SOFT, JUICY RED

BEAUJOLAIS VILLAGES *Domaine Colonge*

2004 (Gamay/Burgundy, France) $37

COTES-DU-RHONE *Domaine Jaume*

"La Friande" 2004 (Grenache Blend/Rhone, France). $33

PINOT NOIR *Beringer*

"Founder's Estate" 2003 (California) $36

SHARP, EARTHY RED

CHIANTI COLLI SENESI *Geografico*

2004 (Sangiovese Blend/Tuscany, Italy). $38

BOURGOGNE ROUGE *Faiveley*

2003 (Pinot Noir/Burgundy, France) $56

PREMIERES COTES DE BORDEAUX *Chateau Duplessy*

2000 (Merlot Blend/Bordeaux, France). $50

STRONG, JAMMY RED

MERLOT *Portal de Alto*

"Gran Reserva" 2003 (Maipo, Chile). $42

ZINFANDEL *Tobin James*

"Ballistic" 2001 (Paso Robles, CA). $50

PETITE SIRAH *Concannon*

2002 (Central Coast, CA). $36

User-Friendly Headings: *By Flavor/Style*

4. HOW EXTENSIVE IS THE LIST?

Bigger is not always better. Tomelike wine lists, while impressive, often leave the diner befuddled and overwhelmed. Unless we're talking about the world's top wine restaurants, a truly helpful wine list will be concise, offering plenty of choices, but shading to the pithy.

5. SPY THE OFFERINGS THEMSELVES.

All restaurants should offer at least a few good bottles that are priced affordably, relative to the menu. If you can't get a bottle for less than the price of two entrées, you'd be right to raise an eyebrow. If most of the offerings resemble those from the fridge of your local convenience store, you're unlikely to be unearthing any buried treasures. Conversely, a diverse by-the-glass list, with some wines you've never heard of, is a positive sign, indicating that the buyer has been scouting for up-and-coming values. This is the kind of place where you can feel secure in broadening your vinous horizons.

M ARNIE'S CORNER

In addition to the wine list, other clues will reveal whether a restaurant really cares about its wine program. At the bar before dinner, check out the stemware. Small glasses served nearly filled are fine for a casual night out, but if we're talking tablecloths and candlelight, you should expect a proper glass that allows room to swirl the wine. Look for evidence of temperature control as well. A glass-fronted wine cabinet inspires more trust than an open-air shelf for reds or whites served icy cold.

HOW TO ACT LIKE YOU KNOW WHAT YOU'RE DOING WHEN ORDERING WINE

FRED DAME
Master Sommelier

D INING OUT IS all about pleasure—good food, good wine, good company. But if you're unsure about the etiquette of wine service, it can be hard to relax and enjoy yourself. Most of us want to project a cool and confident air as hosts, to seem experienced and in control in front of our date or our client. But the first few times we order wine can feel awkward and intimidating. Here are a few tips on what we professionals do when dining out. Try them a few times, and you'll really be experienced and in control (instead of just pretending!).

1. ASK FOR HELP FROM THE SERVICE STAFF, BUT SET BOUNDARIES.

There is no shame in asking a sommelier or server for wine recommendations. No one knows the wine list or the menu better than they. That said, feel free to communicate your limits. There's no need to mention dollars, simply point to an entry and say, "This is what I would normally order, but I'm looking to explore this evening. What can you recommend?" If you are pointing at a wine's price, you'll send a clear message about what you're looking to spend.

Master sommelier **FRED DAME** brings an impressive blend of experience, expertise, and enthusiasm to the world of wine and cuisine. In his role as director of Icon Estates Wine, he assists restaurateurs and hoteliers in developing their wine programs. He founded the American Branch of the Court of Master Sommeliers in 1986 and since that time has played an active role in the expansion of the Master Sommelier program throughout America. He was the first American to serve as president of the Court of Master Sommeliers Worldwide and is currently president of the Guild of Sommeliers Education Foundation.

2. WHEN THE BOTTLE IS PRESENTED AND OPENED, DON'T SMELL THE CORK. WAIT AND SMELL THE WINE.

Cork sniffing is unnecessary. Wine corks smell like tree bark soaked in wine because that's exactly what they are. In theory, the cork's aroma is supposed to indicate the wine's condition, but even for experts, it isn't conclusive. Many wines have flaws that can't be detected from the cork, and perfectly good wines may have off-smelling corks. So why bother? Since many wines now have screw tops and synthetic composites, let's just ignore the closure and focus on the wine.

3. WHEN A TASTE IS POURED FOR YOU, SWIRL THE WINE IN THE GLASS AND SNIFF.

Swirling wine is not an affectation, like pinkies up for sipping tea; the circular action amplifies wine's scent. It can feel awkward, but there's a trick to it: Keep the glass base firmly on the table and move it in circles, not back and forth. Holding the stem as though it were a pencil, "draw" spirals on the tablecloth to send the wine spinning and coat the inside of the bowl. Increased surface area, wet with wine, gives a more intense aroma. Once you've swirled, stick your nose into the bowl and take one or two good sniffs.

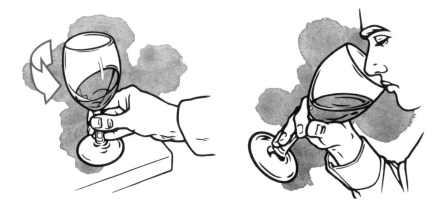

4. IF THE WINE SMELLS GOOD, IT IS GOOD; THERE'S NO NEED TO TAKE A SIP.

Your first sniff will be a better indicator of whether you'll like the wine than your first taste. First sips of wine are often misleading. Typically, they seem too acidic, since the mouth has yet to adjust to the new pH level. Plus, anything recently eaten, drunk, or smoked—from breath mints to scotch to cigars—can alter your perception of the wine, and not always pleasantly. Smell is where the action is with wine, anyway. In fact, our wine enjoyment breaks down to roughly 70 percent smell, 20 percent taste and tactile sensation, and 10 percent visual appreciation. Sniffing wine is a highly accurate preview of flavor, just as smelling is for food. To convey the appearance of being an old hand at wine, just swirl and sniff, don't taste. If the wine smells good, it will automatically taste good.

5. HOLD THE WINEGLASS BY THE STEM OR BASE; DO NOT GRASP THE BOWL.

Wineglasses have "handles" for a reason: to keep hands off the glass bowl. The oils that fingers leave behind can carry strong scents that interfere with wine smells (especially

Correct   *Incorrect*

if you smoke), just as they obscure the wine's clarity. Also, wine is volatile, and small changes in temperature change its flavor dramatically. Even brief contact with hands will quickly heat wine.

6. DISCOVER THE POWER OF THE WORDS "THANK YOU."

There is a misconception that treating restaurant staff poorly—by either ignoring them or being overtly impolite—is somehow "cool" or an indicator of social status. Nothing could be further from the truth. The better traveled and more experienced a guest is, the more likely he or she is to acknowledge the staff and to say "please" and "thank you" graciously. Just remember the golden rule: Do unto others as you would have them do unto you. Simply smiling, making eye contact, and thanking when appropriate is the best investment you can make. As if by magic, the service you receive will improve and all will be well with the world.

MARNIE'S CORNER

Don't hesitate to ask for what you want in restaurant scenarios. The sooner you speak up, the sooner your needs can be met and you can get back to enjoying your evening. Never worry that your request will be an imposition; there's no harm in asking. If what you want is doable, the restaurant should want to do it for you. After all, the more you enjoy your visit, the more likely you are to return. If your request is impossible, they'll tell you so. Are the wineglasses too small to swirl? Ask if they have larger ones. Want to split a wine by the glass or taste it before you commit? Most restaurants will gladly oblige. In top restaurants, you'll often find European-style service, with whites served warmer and reds served cooler than in the average American eatery. If that's not what you prefer, tell your server. He or she will help make it right for you. If you find your white too cold to taste properly, or your red overly warm, tell the server that, too. As a sommelier, I confess, I'm just as likely to have my white on the table and my red on ice as the other way around.

HOW TO GET THE BEST WINE ADVICE IN RESTAURANTS

LARRY STONE
Master Sommelier

S ERVICE IS A large part of what we enjoy when dining out. What is more pleasant than being tended to by people whose job it is to make us happy? At the door and at the table, even in the coatroom or at the valet stand, every form of assistance we might require is provided with a smile. Yet, when it comes to one of the most challenging aspects of dining out—choosing wine—many guests hesitate to take advantage of wine service. Some may not know what resources are available on request. Others may be fearful of asking, perhaps uncertain of wine etiquette or skeptical of the staff's level of expertise. A few may be wary of pressure to spend more on wine, worried that wine service will push their budget beyond its limit. None of these concerns should be a barrier to getting great wine service. If it's at your fingertips, why not indulge?

- **RESTAURANTS WITH A COMMITMENT TO WINE WILL HAVE SOMEONE WELL INFORMED TO DISCUSS SELECTIONS.**
  Not every restaurant will have a sommelier; a dedicated wine steward working the dining room is a luxury rarely found outside the realm of fine dining. But restaurants that make a serious commitment to wine will almost

Master sommelier **LARRY STONE** is general manager of Francis Coppola's Rubicon Estate. He also makes wine in the Napa Valley under the Sirita label. One of the most acclaimed American sommeliers, he is best known for his work at Charlie Trotter's in Chicago and as a partner and wine director of San Francisco's iconic Rubicon restaurant. Stone is the first American to have won the title of International Best Sommelier in French Wines and Spirits by Foods and Wines from France, and he is the only American to have earned the title of French Master Sommelier from the Union de la Sommelerie Française.

always have a knowledgeable wine person on staff. It may be the manager or the owner, a bartender, head server, or perhaps the chef, but even casual venues should have someone to consult if they consider their wine program a strong suit. If you see a well-thought-out wine selection presented crisply and free of typographic errors, or if temperature-controlled wine storage is visible nearby, chances are that a staff member with a degree of wine expertise is available to provide wine service.

- **REQUESTING ADVICE WHEN CHOOSING A WINE IS ALMOST ALWAYS A GOOD IDEA.**
Restaurants are a controlled environment for exploring new styles, places where someone has already selected wines that flatter a particular menu or cuisine. No one will have more familiarity with the specific wines and dishes on the menu than the people who serve them every night. Even servers with less formal training will often know which wines get rave reviews and what really tastes terrific with their signature dish. Our information age has made it easier than ever to learn more about wine; we now see very young professionals and enthusiasts with knowledge that in the past might have taken decades to acquire. Asking for recommendations is usually wise, barring any obvious danger signs, such as shabby or inaccurate wine lists. Of course, caution may be in order if, on a previous visit, aggressive salesmanship has caused you to lose trust in the restaurant.

- **PROVIDE SOME INFORMATION ABOUT YOURSELF IF YOU WANT TO BENEFIT MOST FROM A SOMMELIER'S EXPERTISE.**
If you simply ask for a recommendation, the choice will be based on abstract pairing principles, or perhaps the server's tastes. If you describe your preferences, however, these can be taken into account as well. The simplest means is to tell the server or sommelier what you normally like to drink. Learning a few basic style terms will help you communicate your desires—light or full bodied, sweet or dry. Do you generally prefer California wines over European wines? Do you avoid oaky whites as a rule? If you're more into Pinot Noir than Pinot Grigio, by all means say so. Even if you say you'd like to try something different, knowing something about your style helps the

wine steward decide on a wine you'll love. One important way to determine a server's capability is to gauge his or her knowledge about the wines you've told them you like.

- **ASKING FOR ADVICE DOES NOT REQUIRE CEDING CONTROL OF THE BUDGET.**

  There is widespread fear that wine stewards will try to push customers to spend more than they'd like. Unfortunately, this misperception leads some guests to avoid asking for help when ordering wine. This anxiety is unnecessary. First, most sommeliers are more concerned with making sure their guests are happy and that they leave with a desire to return. Second, as the customer, you're always in the driver's seat, and no one can force you to buy something you don't want. When asked open-endedly, servers generally suggest wines in more than one price range, but that should not be taken as pressure to upgrade. Different guests are looking for different types of experiences, and restaurateurs must please all diners, whether they're energized by bargains or soothed by splurge spending. If you make it clear what you're looking for—by pointing to a comfortable price on the wine list, for example—you'll never feel as though you're getting the hard "upsell." If for whatever reason you don't trust the server about keeping to your budget, and he or she makes recommendations without referring to expense, ask to read the name of the wine on the list so that you can see the price before ordering.

MARNIE'S CORNER

There is no shame in asking for wine assistance; in fact, quite the opposite is true. Dining occasions are often fraught with social expectations; when choosing wine, guests have dates to impress, clients to re-assure, or friends and family to please. The host is expected to be in control, and some are reluctant to ask for help, worried that doing so may smack of weakness. But just as in life, being confident enough to ask for help when you need it is the true sign of strength. Those most knowledgeable about wine—wine professionals and connoisseurs—are more likely than the average diner to seek a sommelier's insights. Asking for wine suggestions does not reflect poorly on a host, any more than does inquiring which pasta a server recommends. Shake that wine anxiety! You're in an establishment that sells wine. What better place to ask for advice and try something new?

HOW TO PICK WINES FOR MULTICOURSE MEALS

RANDY CAPAROSO
Sommelier

RESTAURANTS PROVIDE A wine experience different from the one we encounter at home. At home, we are more comfortable with ourselves, the dishes we prepare, and the wines we offer to our guests. Come and get it! No dealing with the tricky, often tense, formalities of dining out: making reservations, being seated, dealing with the peering eyes of servers and sommeliers.

But I will say this about dining out: It saves you the trouble of washing dishes! In other words, there is no reason that hosting a party in a restaurant, even with multiple courses and wines, should not be simpler than entertaining at home. And it can be, if you follow these guidelines when dining out.

- **THE KEY TO PLANNING A SUCCESSFUL MULTICOURSE WINE EXPERIENCE IN A RESTAURANT IS PREPARATION, ESPECIALLY FOR SPECIAL OCCASIONS.**
  Most restaurants either post their menus and wine lists online or would be happy to mail or fax copies to you. It never hurts to plan ahead. Knowing, for instance, what appetizers and Champagne to order immediately

RANDY CAPAROSO is an award-winning wine professional who has opened restaurants seemingly everywhere, from his original home in the Hawaiian Islands to New York, California, Florida, Illinois, and Texas. He is also a longtime newspaper wine columnist, magazine journalist, and professional wine judge. He currently consults for wineries as well as restaurants.

after sitting down, even before everyone has looked at the menu, will allow you to concentrate more on having fun.

Take it from a restaurateur: For parties of six or more, we love guests who preorder items such as appetizers and wines or, heck, even an entire meal. It's easier for the restaurant, and it's easier for you, too. Don't be afraid to initiate a pre-event conversation with a restaurant.

- **WHEN CHOOSING WINES FOR MULTICOURSE DINING, THE SEQUENCE IN WHICH THEY ARE SERVED IS IMPORTANT.**
The basic guidelines observed in most restaurants are lighter wines before heavier wines, drier wines before sweeter wines, white wines before reds, and sparkling wines before everything else. Usually. When the dishes and the guests dictate that a slightly sweet wine is served before a dry wine, a red wine before a white, or no reds or no whites at all, then that's the best thing to do.

- **SERVING LIGHTER WHITES BEFORE HEAVIER REDS USUALLY MAKES SENSE, BUT THERE ARE EXCEPTIONS.**
We commonly start a meal with salads or seafood appetizers that taste terrific with snappy dry whites such as Sauvignon Blanc or Pinot Grigio. Later, we typically move on to red meat entrées that do better with full-bodied reds, including Merlot or Malbec. Meaty, fatty, often strongly sauced main courses (beef, lamb, or red game) definitely call for the fuller-bodied reds of the world. Why fight it?

But what if the main course is something delicate, perhaps red snapper with lemon butter? Where does a heavy red fit in? It doesn't. Don't be afraid to progress from a lighter white to a fuller-bodied white instead of to a red. An opulent Chardonnay will be just as satisfying with this kind of main course, and far more flattering to the fish. And if your guests truly prefer reds? No problem. There are many lighter red wines that are soft, zesty, and fruity enough to brilliantly match seafood, namely French Beaujolais and Pinot Noirs from California and Oregon.

- **DISHES WITH SWEETNESS OR A SPICY KICK ARE A GREAT REASON TO THINK OF LIGHTLY SWEET WINES.**
Asian cuisine abounds with fun appetizers that feature sweet-tart sauces or a little heat. Off-dry wines such as German Rieslings or fresh and fruity rosés shine with these flavors. Do you love foie gras as much as I do? Well, its sweet accompaniments make this a great excuse to have some dessert in the middle of dinner—dessert wine, that is. Foie gras tastes amazingly delicious with fully sweet wines, like French Sauternes, that are more commonly served after dinner.

- **WHEN IN DOUBT, REMEMBER CHAMPAGNE.**
This versatile style is a sommelier's best friend because it goes with everything. When it comes to starting off an occasion in style, there's nothing like the discreet "pop" of a sparkling wine cork. With or without food, the pure, zesty qualities of dry sparklers are good enough reasons to start with bubbles. The yeast-scented richness of those made in the Champagne method is something special, adding a depth and richness that can take you from salad to steak with grace and panache. Few wines are as flexible with food.

- **DON'T SKIP DESSERT—OR DESSERT WINE. BOTH ARE A GREAT WAY TO CAP OFF A MEMORABLE MEAL.**
When the time comes for dessert, Americans tend to order coffee, not dessert wine. That is a shame because one hasn't really lived until one has experienced, say, a luscious twenty-year-old tawny Port paired with a molten black chocolaty dessert. If you can plan ahead by moderating consumption of wines and foods during the first few courses, you can enjoy the incredible variation of sweet wines from around the world.

MARNIE'S CORNER

Between appetizers and entrées, looking at menus and socializing, dinner in a restaurant can easily take three hours or longer. When people eat out, the stage is set for trying more than one wine, something that rarely makes sense at home. Sommeliers have a lot of practice orchestrating wines to accompany everything from a two-course business lunch to a ten-course chef's tasting menu. Like composing a piece of music or writing a play, we hope to capture interest, build to a climax, and gently ease our guests toward the end of a delightful meal. We try to avoid boring repetition or peaking too soon. The most common progression begins with sparkling wine to pique the appetite, followed by bright whites with appetizers, rich reds with the main course, and a sweet taste of dessert wine that winds down over desserts or cheeses.

HOW TO CHOOSE WINES
FOR A LARGE PARTY

CHRISTIE DUFAULT
Sommelier

C HOOSING A WINE to drink is always easiest at
home. We feel safe and relaxed there, particularly
when we have only our own personal tastes to consider
and a limited number of our favorite bottles to choose
from. If you're the one cooking dinner, you'll also have a
good sense of the food flavors to come. Even if you are
entertaining friends or tasked with bringing the wine for a
dinner party, at least everyone will be eating the same dish,
thus simplifying the choices.

When dining in restaurants, however, the reverse is true
on all counts. The ritual of ordering wine is laden with all
sorts of expectations and complications, and the larger
the party, the more challenging the responsibility. People
want very much to make the "right" choice, but they face
uncertainty on all sides. Wine lists present a wider range of
options than your wine rack at home, and most of the wines
will be unfamiliar. You rarely know exactly how the food
will taste, or even much about your guests' preferences.
Worse still, there's a good chance everyone will order a
different entrée. It's enough to make your head spin.

So, what to do when you need to pick wine for a group
in a restaurant? Sommeliers have practice recommending
crowd-pleasing wines since we serve large parties every

CHRISTIE DUFAULT is a
sommelier and wine consultant based in San Francisco.
Throughout her fifteen-year
career as a sommelier, she
created highly regarded
restaurant wine programs
in esteemed establishments
such as Restaurant Gary
Danko and Quince in San
Francisco and Vincent
Guerithault in Phoenix.
She is also a consultant
for Vintrust, a collectors'
consulting company based
in San Francisco and New
York, and she remains
adjunct faculty at the Rudd
Center for Professional
Wine Studies at the Culinary
Institute of America in the
Napa Valley.

day. With a party of two, we might take a narrower approach, but with a group, first and foremost sommeliers think *versatility*. Here are some insider tips to remember the next time you're in the hot seat, choosing wines for a business dinner or family gathering.

- **FAVOR WINES ON THE LIGHTER, BRIGHTER END OF THE STYLE SPECTRUM THAT DELIVER FLAVOR WITHOUT WEIGHT.**
  Lighter wines are far more versatile than heavier ones. That may sound counterintuitive, since these days wine popularity is driven to a certain degree by intensity and weight. But the ultimate role of wine is to cleanse the palate and enhance the flavor of food, so sommeliers always put the food first. The food experience is special and fleeting and should never be overpowered by a wine partner.

  With many different foods being served with the same wine, it's impossible to avoid a few being mismatched. Erring on the lighter side is far less damaging than the other way around. A rich rack of lamb might cry out for a dense Cabernet Sauvignon, but it will still taste pretty terrific paired with a lighter-weight Chianti. However, the flavors of lighter dishes around the table, such as lemony veal Milanese, chicken quesadillas, or grilled salmon, will be deadened by a heavier wine. Bright, flavorful wines that aren't overly oaky or alcoholic are true crowd pleasers and a win-win for everyone.

  In my restaurant, I recommend lighter styles that are bright and flavorful—for example, sparkling wines and dry rosés, Sauvignon Blancs and Pinot Noirs, Australian Rieslings and Austrian Grüner Veltliners, whites from northern France and northern Italy, and balanced reds from southern France and northern Spain.

- **WITH MORE THAN FOUR PEOPLE, ORDER TWO WINES: ONE RED AND ONE WHITE.**
  You'll likely end up with two bottles anyway, since the average person consumes about two glasses during dinner and each bottle contains five glasses' worth of wine. By ordering both white and red right away, you make certain your guests can drink the style they prefer and can change from one to the other with different courses if they choose.

- **CONSIDER STARTING WITH A BOTTLE OF SPARKLING WINE.
  FOR EIGHT OR MORE PEOPLE, MAKE IT TWO BOTTLES.**
  Sparkling wine is an ideal aperitif. Not only does it taste delicious and cleanse the palate, it stimulates the appetite as well. Ordering a bottle at the start provides your guests with something to drink as they review the menu, and you with more time to scan the wine list. Styles such as rich, toasty French Champagne or Italian Prosecco, with its hint of friendly sweetness, are sure to please even those who might never think to order a glass of bubbly for themselves.

- **WITH DISTINCTIVE CUISINES, CONSIDER THE DOMINANT
  FOOD THEME.**
  Most restaurants cover a wide range of flavor bases, but some specialize more tightly. For example, you might want to tilt toward subtler wines at the sushi bar or oakier wines at the smokehouse.

- **GIVE THE SERVICE STAFF THE GREEN LIGHT TO OPEN BOTTLES
  AS NEEDED, WITHIN REASON.**
  Approving and tasting every bottle will slow service, but giving blanket permission to keep the wine flowing can result in more opened wine than is necessary. For large groups, you can expect to consume roughly one bottle for every two guests. Let your server or sommelier know to open wine as needed but to check in with you once you've consumed a specified number of bottles.

MARNIE'S CORNER

For the largest gatherings, avoid extremes of style and gravitate toward the middle. Think of it as the "Goldilocks Rule": not too light, not too heavy, not too sweet, not too dry—just right. When you're entertaining more than twenty people, it's hard to go wrong with styles whose strong suit is moderation. Midweight wines are the way to go to please most of the people most of the time; Italian Pinot Grigio will have wider appeal than whisper-light Vinho Verde or heavier Chardonnay. The same applies to flavor profile: Red wines with a midrange dark fruit flavor, such as Merlot or Shiraz, will be better received than a sharp cranberry-ish Bourgogne or a dense, raisiny, old vine Zinfandel.

HOW, WHEN, AND WHY
TO SEND BACK A BOTTLE
OF WINE

PIERO SELVAGGIO
Restaurateur

WINE RITUALS IN restaurants can be mystifying. When hosts order a bottle, they are always offered a taste to approve the wine before it is poured for their guests. Many people are confused about what they should look for when asked to judge the wine and are afraid to ask. Some are too shy to reject a bottle, worrying that to do so is rude. Others misunderstand the purpose of the sample taste, sending bottles back for little or no reason. Neither of these extremes is correct. Wine should be rejected only if it is truly bad or if it was recommended in error.

Since wine is a natural product, each and every bottle is unique. Like grapes, a few wines are imperfect. Wine can be damaged by many factors, most often faulty corks, poor storage, and accidents of winemaking. Although modern winemaking has greatly reduced the number of disappointing bottles, many reasons can cause a wine to be unfit to serve your guests.

PIERO SELVAGGIO is founder and owner of the Valentino Restaurant Group and one of the modern fathers of Italian cuisine in America. In 1972, with limited funds and only a modest culinary background, he opened a small Italian restaurant in an unglamorous Santa Monica neighborhood. More than thirty years later Valentino—one of the finest restaurants in the Los Angeles area as well as the nation—is known for its exceptional focus on wine. Selvaggio's hospitality family has grown to include restaurants in Las Vegas and on the seven seas, with Crystal Cruises.

- **GUESTS ARE ASKED TO SAMPLE EACH BOTTLE OF WINE BECAUSE SOME BOTTLES ARE DEFECTIVE.**
No restaurateur wants guests to suffer through a spoiled wine any more than a burnt risotto. It's not good for business. If there is a problem with anything you're served, including the wine, you should always speak up. Don't be embarrassed. You are doing the restaurant a favor by giving them a chance to correct the situation.

- **WINE CAN HAVE UNUSUAL FLAVORS, ESPECIALLY ON THE FIRST SIP, SO TAKE YOUR TIME AND TRUST YOUR NOSE.**
Wines can seem one way alone and then change personality with food. Also, the palate takes a sip or two to adjust to wine. Don't immediately assume that something's wrong just because a wine has an uncommon aroma or seems too acidic. With wine, it's always wise to pay more attention to your nose than to your mouth. Even great wines can smell a little strange—earthy or leathery or leafy and so on. Interesting smells are okay, but if a wine's smell crosses the line into unappetizing, it will rarely taste good.

- **CORK TAINT IS THE MOST COMMON CAUSE FOR WINE TO BE REJECTED; SUCH WINES ARE SAID TO BE "CORKED."**
No, a corked wine is not one with pieces of cork floating in it. We use this term for wines that have an offensive smell because of a bad cork, similar to the smell of a mildewed basement after a flood. Corks are made from the bark of a tree and can host microorganisms. Ironically, the unpleasant-smelling compound known as TCA can also be caused by treatments intended to clean the corks. Wines may be only faintly corked or badly corked. In addition to the presence of unpleasant aromas, corked wines may also suffer from a marked absence of the "good" aromas a wine should have. There is little agreement about what percentage of wines are corked, with estimates ranging from 1 percent to 10 percent. What is certain is that more flawed wine is drunk in restaurants than good wine is returned. So if you suspect a wine is off, ask the wine steward for his or her opinion.

- **WINES THAT HAVE BEEN POORLY STORED OR AGED TOO LONG MAY ALSO BE COMPROMISED ENOUGH TO DESERVE REJECTION.**
  Although this problem has become much less common, it is still possible to find bottles that are oxidized from cracked or dried-out corks. These wines may have a sour smell of rotten fruit. Wines that are past their prime, or those that have been exposed to too much heat or light, can smell tired and almost malty, a particularly common problem for half-bottles. Unpleasant smells of vinegar, roasted nuts, or burnt rubber are also signs of problems. Wines by the glass that have been open too long sometimes smell completely flat or taste of the refrigerator.

- **IT IS RARE, BUT POSSIBLE, FOR AN ERROR OF SERVICE TO RUIN A BOTTLE OF WINE.**
  If a sommelier accidentally tops off glasses with the wrong wine, he or she should remove the bottle and bring another. The same is true if the glass neck is somehow cracked or broken when opening the bottle.

- **THERE IS ONLY ONE CIRCUMSTANCE IN WHICH YOU SHOULD SEND WINE BACK SIMPLY BECAUSE IT DOESN'T SUIT YOUR TASTES.**
  If you trusted the advice of a server or sommelier and the wine chosen for you is truly not to your liking, you do not need to accept the recommendation. It was your server's duty to determine what you would like, and not just to assume you'd share his or her tastes. If your server didn't ask you about your tastes, he or she had little to go on. Speak up right away, and your server will gladly bring a replacement.

MARNIE'S CORNER

Within the wine industry there is much debate about corks and cork taint. Corks have served vintners well for centuries, and they have shaped how we age and store wine. But corks clearly have a failure rate that is too high for comfort. Worse, very few wine drinkers notice cork problems when they do encounter them. The wine might simply not impress them as much as it should. This is just as damaging to the vintner as an overtly bad bottle. What business can afford to have such inconsistency, the variation from bottle to bottle that is unavoidable with corks? Many wineries have changed to alternative closures, from screw tops to synthetic corks. These new technologies are an attempt to improve consistency and provide the customer with a better wine experience.

CHAPTER
SIX

Wine at Home

HOME IS WHERE WE EAT MOST OF OUR MEALS AND DRINK MOST OF OUR WINE. BUT SINCE WINE CAN SEEM SO COM-PLICATED, EVEN REGULAR DRINKERS MAY FEEL LESS comfortable serving wine to their guests than when serving other drinks. Most of us don't have wine cellars for storing dozens of bottles or side-boards for dozens of wineglasses, nor should we need to. It's just a beverage, after all.

Wine is a unique agricultural product, in many ways closer to produce or cheese than to vodka or whiskey. Unlike other drinks, it occupies a strange limbo between the perishable items chilled in the refrigerator and the dry goods stored in the cupboard. Beer doesn't keep well, so we know to buy small amounts and keep it fresh. Spirits are stable enough so that we don't worry about the bottles spoiling after they've been opened. But wine can be perplexing. Some wines can keep very well for years or even decades, whereas others are best consumed when fresh. Yet, they can all be easily damaged with too much heat or light. The serving of wine can be more puzzling still. Beer and cocktails may be sipped from nearly any vessel, but wine benefits greatly when served in specialized glassware. Service temperature dramatically affects wine's nuance and aromatics, too.

There is no question that serving wine presents a bit of a challenge. But whether your family enjoys wine regularly or only when entertaining guests, getting a handle on a few basic concepts will help. Learning a little about how wine works—how it keeps, how it spoils, how to showcase it—will allow us to feel more comfortable with it in our homes everyday as well as when pulling a cork on a bottle to share with guests.

HOW TO PRESERVE OPEN WINE

(YES, YOU CAN FREEZE IT)

─────◆◆═◆◆─────

RONN WIEGAND
Master of Wine & Master Sommelier

───

OFTEN WE FIND ourselves with more wine than we need and would like to enjoy the rest another time. A half-finished bottle will never taste the same the next day, let alone a week later. If we want to preserve opened wine, we must take steps to protect it. Unlike vodka or vinaigrette, wine cannot be sealed up and expected to remain unchanged.

Wine is not inert; its flavor begins to shift as soon as the seal is broken. Wine changes as it matures at the winery and ages in cellared bottles. It even changes while in the glass as we drink it. These chemical changes irreversibly alter the wine itself, not simply our perception of it (as service temperature or food context might). Most of these changes are driven by exposure to air and the oxygen it contains.

Many gadgets and treatments on the market claim to preserve opened wine by blocking or slowing the impact of oxygen. However, none are capable of making wine taste exactly as it did on pulling the cork, and even those products that are effective will not work indefinitely. Wine is a volatile, organic product and never "stands still."

RONN WIEGAND is both a master of wine and master sommelier, the first in the world to hold both prestigious titles. A widely published author with thirty-five years of wine industry experience, he is founder and publisher of the hospitality journal *Restaurant Wine*. His *TasteTour* series of intuitive wine guides and charts are recognized as essential tools of the trade. In 2008, he introduced a line of lead-free crystal wineglasses of his own design, the Signature Series from Germany's Eisch Glaskultur. He also offers consulting services and has been a wine instructor at Napa Valley College since 1988.

- **AIR CHANGES WINE. TOO MUCH WILL DEGRADE IT, BUT SMALL AMOUNTS HELP SOME STYLES REACH THEIR FULL POTENTIAL.**
Winemakers carefully calibrate wine's exposure to air. Porous oak barrels allow wine to slowly "breathe"—a benefit for many wine styles. The changes that we can taste as bottled wines mature are driven by air also, by interaction with the small amount trapped within the bottle. In both circumstances, oxidation is the primary force, proceeding at a snail's pace to slowly alter the wine. But when the cork is removed and wine is poured, the rush of oxygen-rich air triggers rapid and irreversible changes.

  With fine wines that have yet to reach their prime, these changes can be positive; the wine may actually improve for a day or two. However, degradation after opening is far more common. In addition to oxidation, exposure to air allows bacteria to begin converting alcohol into acetic acid. The first steps on this road to wine vinegar can become noticeable within a few days.

- **NOT ALL WINE STYLES CAN BE PRESERVED. SOME ARE RESIL-IENT; OTHERS ARE MORE FRAGILE.**
Subtle wines generally suffer most quickly, as with many lighter whites. Bolder flavors have the best chance of lasting, such as those found in young full-bodied reds. Sparkling wines generally won't hold up after opening since only special stoppers and high-tech equipment can keep them from losing effervescence. Most wines aged ten years or more should also be consumed immediately, for they have already been partially oxidized and will quickly lose their fragrance and charm.

- **REFRIGERATION MAY HELP PRESERVE OTHER FOODS BUT CAN SPEED THE DECLINE OF WINE.**
The general rule is that cold preserves and heat degrades, but with wine another factor comes into play. Refrigeration does slow the oxidation process but also renders oxygen more soluble. The fridge may be better than a hot countertop next to the stove, but a cool pantry is an even better bet for storing opened wine.

- **VACUUM DEVICES ARE A WASTE OF TIME. THEY SIMPLY DO NOT WORK.**
  The vacuum theory may sound sensible, but it's based on faulty logic. Pumping out air may slow wine's conversion to vinegar somewhat, but creating a vacuum in the bottle replaces one problem with another. The change in pressure in the headspace will suck oxygen and other components from the wine to fill the void. Unfortunately, this includes volatile esters—the source of wine's aroma. By stripping scent from wine, vacuum preservation eviscerates flavor, thereby diminishing the wine's character.

- **TOP RESTAURANTS RELY ON INERT GASES (NITROGEN OR ARGON) TO PRESERVE OPEN WINE.**
  Restaurants with extensive "by the glass" programs require effective wine preservation. Many use complex gas-preservation systems and equipment for serving wine "on tap," as for draught beer. Others simply "sparge" their open bottles regularly with inert gas. In both cases, nitrogen or argon are used to displace air and function as a protective blanket. This system is reliable and can extend a wine's life by a few days and, sometimes, up to two or three weeks. Spray cans for home use are widely available but feel empty even when full, and therefore they can be confusing to use.

- **FREEZING WINE IS THE MOST EFFECTIVE METHOD AND ALLOWS OPEN WINE TO BE KEPT FOR MONTHS OR EVEN YEARS.**
  I know it sounds ridiculous, but for more than thirty years, I've been freezing opened wine, with incredible results. The "Wiegand method" has a few limitations: The bottles must be upright, the cork must be clean, and some harmless sediment will form during freezing. But there is no denying that it works. Freezing is capable of preserving everything from White Zinfandel to Château d'Yquem, with chilling efficiency. As with other methods, young wines are most resilient, and reds tend to last longer than whites. Thawing a frozen bottle takes a few hours, but I prefer the convenience of a few moments in the microwave. As long as you have the freezer space to spare, freezing is the only way I know to preserve opened wine not just for days, but weeks, months, or even years.

MARNIE'S CORNER

The more "empty" space in the bottle, the faster open wine will decline. One solution is to displace the air in the bottle or transfer the contents to a smaller container. In laboratories, clean glass marbles are used to bring a wine's fill level back to the top. This method is hardly practical at home, though, as it makes pouring a glass a challenge. Putting the wine in a smaller bottle achieves a similar effect. Save half and quarter bottles or even resealable glass iced-tea bottles. Make sure that both the bottle and the closure are clean, and gently pour down the side to avoid needlessly stirring up the wine. This method will slow the impact of air but won't stop it entirely. Changing bottles does make the wine hard to identify, so you may want to make a note somewhere or mark the new container.

HOW TO SERVE AND STORE WINE AT THE RIGHT TEMPERATURE

MARK SQUIRES
Wine Writer

NEWCOMERS TO WINE encounter all sorts of "rules." Some of the most complicated—and important—relate to temperature. Temperature is important in serving and storing wine for the same two reasons it's important in serving and storing other natural foods. Wine tastes different at different temperatures, and temperature affects how long it will keep. Proper storage conditions will significantly extend a wine's shelf-life.

Whites are often served well chilled, frequently in the 35°F to 40°F (2°C to 4°C) range that is standard for refrigerators, whereas reds are supposed to be served at room temperature, roughly 70°F to 75°F (21°C to 24°C). In practice, however, the rules of thumb lead people to serve many whites too cold and many reds too hot. Cold anaesthetizes our ability to perceive wine's flavors. Until they warm up a little, ice-cold white wines can seem tasteless. By contrast, when too warm, reds may seem overly alcoholic and clumsy. The old maxim about serving red wines at room temperature doesn't take into account that many modern homes are kept too warm for properly storing wine. Temperature control is so important for storing wine that top wine merchants and importers often

MARK SQUIRES reviews wines for Robert Parker's *Wine Advocate*, covering Portugal's dry wines as well as the wines of Israel, Greece, Lebanon, Cyprus, Bulgaria, and Romania. He also teaches, consults, and writes on wine in Philadelphia and through his own Web site. He hosts Mark Squires' Bulletin Board, one of the wine world's most popular online forums for discussing wine.

advertise the temperature of their warehouse facilities or shipping containers; some even refrigerate their wine stores to a chilly cellar temperature of 56°F (13°C).

- **WINE FLAVOR IS HIGHLY SENSITIVE TO TEMPERATURE.**
  Ice cold wines will taste bland and flavorless. They seem lighter and aromatically muted, whereas warmer wines seem stronger, sweeter, and bolder. As temperatures creep up into the mid-70s, alcohol begins to evaporate much more quickly, giving wines an unpleasantly boozy smell that sears the nose and throat.

- **TYPICALLY, THE MOST DELICATE WINES ARE SERVED COOLER, WHEREAS MORE ROBUST WINES ARE SERVED WARMER.**
  This general rule means cold whites and warm reds, but uncommonly strong whites or light reds can change the tables. It is a matter of taste, and it is impossible to generalize without taking the specific wine into account, but big reds rarely show well at temperatures past the upper 60s and low 70s (18°C to 24°C). Tastes will differ among individuals, but for me somewhere around 65°F to 70°F (18°C to 21°C) often seems ideal. Lighter reds such as Beaujolais might be chilled even a little more. Whites do well in a 50°F to 60°F range (10°C to 15°C). Sparkling wines tend to be best served coldest of all, since they lose finesse and flatten quickly as they warm.

- **FOR STORING WINE, COLD SLOWS WINE'S DEVELOPMENT, AND HEAT SPEEDS IT UP.**
  We've known for centuries that cold is a preservative. As with food in the refrigerator, the changes that take place in wine as it matures are slowed in cold storage. For mid- to long-term storage, temperatures near 56°F (13°C) are generally considered "classic" for wine cellars, where wine can age best and longest. There is nothing wrong with storing wines somewhat warmer as long as the temperature is constant. In fact, some people prefer the temperature to be in the low 60s, so that the wine will not take as long to evolve in the cellar.

  However, if the temperature reaches the 70s or if fluctuations of temperature start to occur, the wine is more at risk. At warmer temperatures, wine's flavor development progresses less gracefully, and freshness is quickly lost. Fruit flavors begin to tire prematurely, seeming dried or cooked. Wines stored colder than cellar temperature will not be damaged as long as they are not inadvertently frozen, but they also will not develop properly in the long term.

- **FOR MOST WINE LOVERS, KEEPING WINE IN THE FRIDGE OR A COOL PLACE IS MORE THAN ADEQUATE IN THE SHORT TERM.**
  Unless you're storing bottles like a squirrel hoarding nuts, chances are you don't need a wine cellar or specialized cooler. Most wine drinkers open the bottle within a few days of purchase or at most a few weeks. Besides, the vast majority of modern wines are designed to enjoy immediately, not to improve over years of bottle aging. As long as your home isn't swelteringly hot, the basement, a cool closet, or the refrigerator should work well for short-term storage, that is, days or weeks. Some types of wines, including Champagnes, tend to be more fragile than others, such as Port or Barolo.

  It is an unhappy reality, however, that the best wines can age for a long time and are often at their best after long aging. Yet, most people struggle to find some way to care for them properly. If you have begun accumulating bottles that you're saving for a special occasion or that you hope to mature before enjoying them, face the inevitable: You need a wine cooler, a wine cellar, or space in an off-site storage facility. There is no point in buying great wines to cellar if you cannot protect them.

MARNIE'S CORNER

Not everyone agrees about what tastes best, and only you can decide what you like. Efforts to reach proper serving temperature are only worthwhile if doing so helps you take more pleasure from your wine. Personally, I find that pulling my whites out of the fridge ten minutes before I plan to serve them and popping my reds in ten minutes before I plan to serve them is the perfect way to maximize my flavor enjoyment. But if you'd like to zap the winter chill off your wine by popping it in the microwave? Knock yourself out. If you'll like it better with a few ice cubes, so be it. To be honest, I know of at least one famous California vintner who loves to drink his luxe Cabernet Sauvignon on the rocks. It's your wine. Feel free to do whatever is necessary to enjoy it.

HOW TO CHOOSE AN ALL-PURPOSE WINEGLASS

TARA Q. THOMAS
Wine Author

WINEGLASSES ARE IMPORTANT, but they can be taken too seriously. Good wine will taste good, no matter what you drink it from. If all you have are coffee mugs, they'll work just fine. Is it true that wine tastes better in a wineglass? Sure. But should you forgo drinking wine if you don't have the fancy crystal? No way. In fact, many wine-drinking regions of Europe manage perfectly well serving wine in tumblers.

However, it is nice to have a decent set of stemware at home. Proper glasses help us appreciate wine with all the senses, much the way a movie benefits from a big screen in a hushed, darkened theater. Don't worry about shopping for specialized stemware for every style of wine, though. One all-purpose glass will do perfectly well for everything from white to red, Champagne to Port. As an added bonus, sticking to one glass means that you can get more of them, so you'll have enough when friends come over.

The best wineglass is one that feels comfortable and allows us to appreciate every aspect of the wine inside, from its color to its taste and texture. Here are a few tips.

TARA Q. THOMAS is an award-winning wine writer and editor-in-chief for *Wine and Spirits* magazine. She is also the author of *The Complete Idiot's Guide to Wine Basics*, a refreshingly simple take on the wine primer. She specializes in the wines of the Mediterranean and teaches about wine at Mise-en-Place cooking school in downtown Denver. Thomas also serves as wine editor for the *Denver Post*, where she writes a biweekly column for the nation's fifth largest Sunday newspaper.

1. STICK TO PLAIN, CLEAR GLASSES.

Wine is beautiful; it doesn't need any help. Simple and unadorned glasses are your best bet. Color schemes may be fun and cut glass can be pretty, but decoration makes it hard to see the contents.

2. FIND A GLASS WHOSE STEM FEELS COMFORTABLE IN YOUR HAND.

Stems may seem pretentious, but they actually serve a practical purpose. Like handles on teacups, stems keep our hands off the bowl. We won't muck up the glass with grubby fingerprints or warm the wine too quickly with our hot little mitts. Most important, the stem allows for easy swirling, which liberates wine's aromas. Since most of what we perceive as flavor is in fact smell, swirling helps get the most pleasure from your wine, much the way stirring a pot of soup makes it easier to get a whiff.

Ideally, a glass should be tall enough that your hand fits comfortably below the bowl. However, if your dishwasher eats stems for breakfast, you may want to go shorter or even stemless. It's most important to find a glass from which you feel comfortable drinking. Even the most beautiful glass will stay in the cupboard if you're scared to handle it.

3. LOOK FOR A PEAR-SHAPED BOWL THAT NARROWS TOWARD THE TOP.

Like snifters, wineglasses are designed to be swirled without splashing. The key is to have a glass that is widest near the bottom. It should also be large enough so that you can fill it with a decent portion and still leave at least a few inches between the surface of the wine and the rim of the glass.

4. YOUR GLASS SHOULD BE LESS THAN HALF FULL.

Those gigantic red-wine glasses, the ones large enough to stick your head in? Unnecessary. A glass that holds 10 to 12 ounces total is just right. The ideal is a pear-shaped glass large enough to hold a 3-ounce portion of wine yet still be no more than one-third full, with the liquid usually at or near the widest point of the bowl. This allows for easy swirling without sloshing wine all over your shirt, and it provides enough room to capture ample aromas in the headspace.

5. LOOK FOR THE THINNEST RIM THAT IS STILL PRACTICAL.

Modest glasses have thick and rounded rims to make them sturdier. Better glasses have a cut rim that's much thinner. These are a little more fragile, but they're worth it: You'll barely feel the glass on your lips. It's like the difference between sheer, silk long underwear and thick, bulky woolens.

6. IF YOU DO SPRING FOR A SECOND TYPE OF GLASS, MAKE IT A CHAMPAGNE FLUTE.

An all-purpose glass is all you really need for whites and reds, rosés and dessert wines. It will even do for Champagne, but you may find it's worth the splurge for a few tall flutes. These tall, thin glasses not only show off the bubbles in a sparkling wine, they help them last longer, too. Less surface area means less opportunity for the bubbles to dissipate. Besides, they look gorgeous.

MARNIE'S CORNER

I'm often asked if the super-duper wineglasses with shapes tailored to specific grapes and styles really improve the experience. Of course they do. I should hope so, since top-of-the-line stems can be quite costly. Then again, a Ferrari handles better than a Toyota. Whether it makes sense for you to buy one is another question entirely.

It's telling that centuries ago, when stemware was first commercially available, it was viewed as a status symbol. Crystal is beautiful but fragile, and desperately impractical as well. Owning one set was a sign of wealth; owning many conveyed serious prestige. Not much has changed. Unless you're a globe-trotting millionaire, a single wineglass shape will do perfectly well. At home, I prefer to serve everything in a nice 12-ounce white-wine glass.

HOW TO USE LEFTOVER
WINE IN THE KITCHEN

JACQUES PÉPIN
Chef

WINE IS VERY much a part of the dining experience, not just something to drink to kill thirst. To me, wine is inseparable from eating well, but it can also be useful in the kitchen. Wine is a liquid that doesn't dilute taste and that comes in many styles. Wine can bring as much pungent flavor to a recipe as a rich stock. Its acidity is similar to the tang of vinegar or citrus, only milder and less aggressive.

Growing up in France, wine was a staple, served with every meal. This everyday wine had no "color." We weren't choosing a style to "match" our dinner, we drank the local red wine—Beaujolais or Côtes-du-Rhône. We cooked with the wine and served it with our meals, of course. When we reached the bottom of our cask in the cellar, my mother used the dregs and sediment to make stew.

Wine is a key ingredient, another seasoning for the chef. For those who find themselves with wine leftovers at home, there are many ways to incorporate it into your own cooking. But I confess that in my house, wine is not left over very often. We do a good job of finishing most bottles we open.

One of America's best-known chefs and cookbook authors, **JACQUES PÉPIN** has published 25 cookbooks and hosted nine acclaimed public television cooking series. His latest book, a visual biography entitled *Chez Jacques: Traditions and Rituals of a Cook*, contains one hundred of his favorite recipes, showcases his art and essays on food history and cooking, and includes stunning photographs of him enjoying life with family and friends. Pépin's recent PBS series include *The Complete Pépin, Fast Food My Way*, and *More Fast Food My Way*, all produced by San Francisco's KQED and paired with companion cookbooks.

- **IF A WINE TASTES BAD, DON'T COOK WITH IT.**
Cooking will not improve the flavor of bad wine. If the wine was once good but simply tastes faded or flattened, don't worry. It has just been open too long, and it will be fine for use in the kitchen. However, mildew smells are a sign of a common wine problem known as cork taint that will taste just as bad in your recipe. Instead of cooking with them, take such wines back to your wine merchant to exchange them for fresh bottles.

- **IF A WINE TASTES VERY GOOD, DON'T COOK WITH IT.**
I am a chef, not a sommelier, but cooking is a waste of great wine. If a wine can be savored and appreciated, drink it. A sauce made with world-class Châteauneuf-du-Pape will not taste so different from one made with a modest Côtes-du-Rhône. Also, the finest wines are so well made that many will continue to taste very good for days after being opened. Some may surprise you by tasting even better. Taste leftover wine before sending it to the saucepan.

- **COOKING REDUCES WINE, CONCENTRATING FLAVOR AND REMOVING ALCOHOL.**
With heat, wine reduces quickly as alcohol and water vaporize, leaving everything else behind. Whatever flavors were present in the wine will grow stronger in the liquid that remains. Sweet wines will get sweeter, fruity wines fruitier, herbal-scented wines more herbal, and so on. Alcohol is more volatile than water and evaporates faster, but it will not burn off completely. A small fraction will always be present in the final dish.

- **WINE MARINADES KEEP FISH MOIST AND TENDERIZE MEATS.**
Wine makes a great marinade for fish, a flavorful means of adding moisture to low-fat fish, which can dry out easily in cooking. Also, wine's acidity brightens flavor, just like a squeeze of lemon or a splash of vinegar. For meats, wine provides another benefit. Exposure to wine's acidity will soften toughness when used in marinades or in braising liquids.

- **FINISHING WITH A SPLASH OF WINE REFRESHES THE FLAVOR OF A DISH.**
Wine assumes depth and richness when cooked into a sauce or a stew, but it also loses freshness. Although it is best to cook in the wine long enough to eliminate its "raw" alcoholic taste, a small jigger of the same wine added at the last minute will awaken the layers of wine flavor in a pleasant way.

MARNIE'S CORNER

Recipes are made to be changed. Whipping up something different and exploring new flavors is more than half the fun. If you're looking for a healthy way to experiment, wine makes a great flavorful, low-fat substitute for other common ingredients. When poaching fish or making soup, supplement the water with white wine to add a different taste. When sautéing vegetables or meats, replace the majority of the oil with red wine and simmer to lighten the dish without sacrificing flavor. Wine and a splash of oil can pinch-hit for a rich stock or broth. For a nutty, complex flavor, try finishing a sauce or stew with a spoonful of fortified wine such as Madeira or Sherry, instead of butter. Even in baking, wine can be used in place of half the fat in many dessert recipes, with delicious results.

HOW TO SAFELY OPEN A BOTTLE OF CHAMPAGNE

CHARLES CURTIS
Master of Wine

S PARKLING WINE HAS long been associated with celebration and can set a festive mood for any occasion. Synonymous with luxury, French Champagne is the cream of the crop. Not only is it an ideal aperitif, it also acts as a food wine par excellence, contributing an exciting accompaniment to many types of cuisine. In fact, there's a saying among sommeliers: "When in doubt, pair Champagne."

Champagne may be perfect for entertaining, but many are nervous when opening the bottle. Although no corkscrew or special tool is required, the bottles feature a pressurized cork and a wire cage that may be intimidating. For the savvy drinker, it is well worth learning how to open and serve sparkling wine like a pro. You do need to be careful, but there's no need to be fearful. And if opening a Champagne bottle causes a little anxiety the first few times you try, rest assured there's a simple way to solve that problem: Pour yourself a glass and relax.

1. CHILL THE CHAMPAGNE.

Always begin with a bottle that's chilled but not iced (45°F–50°F; 7°C–10°C). If the wine is too warm, the cork will eject too forcefully and the wine will foam up and

CHARLES CURTIS is a master of wine and vice president and head of wine sales for the legendary English auction house Christie's, where he oversees North American wine sales. Originally trained as a chef, Curtis graduated from Le Cordon Bleu Paris and apprenticed at the Crillon Hotel and La Grande Cascade before embarking on a restaurant career in the United States. Since entering the wine trade in 1994, he has worked in several sales positions for importers and distributors and most recently served as director of wine and spirit education for Moët Hennessy USA.

make a mess. Shaking the bottle before opening will have a similar effect. Most of us would rather drink our Champagne than wear it, so unless you've just won the Super Bowl or the World Cup, this is not a good idea. Chilling reduces internal pressure, making bottles of bubbly safe and easy to open. If the contents are too cold, however, the Champagne's delicate and complex flavors will be muted.

2. REMOVE THE FOIL AND SECURE THE CORK.

Remove the foil to expose the cork and wire cage. Most sparkling wines have a pull tab that makes this easy. Hold the neck of the bottle in your left hand, with your index finger or thumb pressing down on the metal cap. Be sure to maintain control of the cork, or it might pop out at high speed. Once the cage is loosened, you won't be able to let go. You don't want to put anyone's eye out with a flying Champagne cork!

3. LOOSEN THE CAGE AND THEN SWITCH HANDS.

With your right hand, grasp the loop of wire that holds the cork in tightly. Untwist it (six and a half turns is usually enough). Loosen the cage completely, but do not remove it. Next, transfer the bottle neck to your right hand without ever relinquishing control of the cork. With your right hand, firmly grasp both cage and cork together and hold steady, shifting your left hand to the bottom of the bottle.

4. TURN THE BOTTLE TO LOOSEN AND EASE OUT THE CORK.

Rotate the bottle a slow quarter turn to loosen the cork. At this point, the cork will try to pop out on its own—don't let it! Although a big pop sounds joyous and will get people's attention, avoiding this noise will keep more bubbles in the wine. Exert pressure on the cork with your right hand to stop it from jumping out, and gently ease it noiselessly out of the bottle.

5. POUR AND ENJOY!

Gently pour the wine into Champagne flutes or white-wine glasses. Residue of oils or detergent can flatten the wine's "sparkle," so make sure the glasses are pristine.

Figure A. Remove the foil.

Figure B. Hold the neck of the bottle in your left hand, with your thumb or index finger pressing down on the metal cap. Loosen the cage.

Figure C. Turn the bottle to loosen the cork.

Figure D. Pour and enjoy!

MARNIE'S CORNER

Sparkling wines of all kinds are a delight, providing a terrific way to help your guests shed the day's cares. Carbonation speeds the absorption of alcohol into the bloodstream, so it's little wonder they make such a popular aperitif. From the simple fruity freshness of Italian Prosecco to the nutty character of Spanish Cava, and from the liqueur-like richness of California sparklers to the toasty elegance of French Champagne, sparkling wine is an ideal way to start the night off right. There is a misconception, however, that sparkling wines are best consumed with sweet things, whether paired with dessert or served with berries in the glass. Be careful: Sweet food will make sparkling wines taste tarter and less sweet, enough to set your teeth on edge. Sweet sparklers such as Italian Asti, Moscato, or Brachetto are better bets in this context than traditional dry "Brut" bubblies, which are far better with savory foods.

HOW TO GET A HANDLE
ON MATURE WINES

MICHAEL MARTINI
Winemaker

I'M ASKED A lot of questions about "old wines," especially how to tell if they're still good. It comes with the territory, given my family business. My grandfather opened his own winery in 1933, and over the years the wines that he and my father made have proven surprisingly long-lived. I've had the pleasure of drinking them on many occasions. When they're well kept, they're like old friends—a window into my family's past. But I'll be the first to admit that not all wines keep well, and old wines are not automatically better than young ones.

The truth is that most wines do not improve with long-term aging, and many of the few that do will have been matured at the winery and taste their best upon release. All wines need a little maturation after fermentation, usually at least three to six months, to rest and allow their flavors to emerge. Some styles benefit from months or even years of maturing in barrels before bottling. In both cases, this is done before the wines are shipped to wine stores. Bottle-aging *after* release is another matter.

The vast majority of wines are designed to be consumed within five years of release. Very old wines, like aged cheeses, are an acquired taste; not everyone likes the changes that take place. Over time, fresh fruity flavors

MICHAEL "MIKE" MARTINI learned the subtle arts of winemaking and grape growing firsthand working alongside his father and grandfather at his family's winery in the Napa Valley. After earning a degree in fermentation science at the University of California at Davis, he became winemaker at the Louis M. Martini winery, carrying his family's traditions into the third generation. He is a past president of the Napa Valley Vintners' Association, an organization his grandfather helped establish. When not making wine, Martini enjoys riding his Harley-Davidson motorcycle and playing guitar in a winemakers' rock band called "Private Reserve."

seem more stewed or dried. New flavors emerge, often funky or earthy, as complex chemical reactions occur. Wines move away from such flavors as fresh fruit and toward flavors more similar to tea, cigars, or wild mushrooms.

- **WINES ARE DAMAGED BY HEAT, LIGHT, AND ARID CONDITIONS.**
Dark, cool, damp cellars are ideal for preserving wine. Underground temperatures hover at or near 55°F (13°C). Just like fresh produce, wine will quickly spoil when stored in warm temperatures or exposed to sunlight. Moisture is important, since most wines are sealed with natural cork. Wine is stored on its side to prevent the corks from drying out; a shriveled cork may allow air into the bottle.

- **BOTTLE SIZE WILL AFFECT A WINE'S ABILITY TO AGE. THE LARGER THE BOTTLE, THE MORE SLOWLY IT WILL MATURE.**
Regardless of the bottle's size, roughly the same amount of airspace will exist between the wine and the cork. Because this air plays a critical role in bottle aging, the ratio of air to wine is important. Half bottles peak quickly and begin to degrade quickly as well, because they have twice as much air for every ounce of wine. For any given wine, the biggest bottles made, such as a magnum, jeroboam, or methuselah, will have the longest lifespan.

- **FADED LABELS AND MOLDY CORKS DO NOT INDICATE A SPOILED WINE, BUT SEEPING CORKS AND LOW FILL LEVELS ARE DANGER SIGNS.**
Bottles kept in dark, moist cellars will often look compromised—faded, dusty, or spotted with mold. None of these problems affect the wine stored inside. In fact, these are good signs and suggest proper storage. However, sticky drips near the cork indicate that the wine may have experienced excessive heat, and low fill levels (especially below the bottle neck) may suggest a seal that is less than perfect. In both cases, the wine might still be good, but the odds are against it.

- **COLOR CHANGES WITH AGING AND CAN BE THE MOST RELIABLE INDICATOR OF WHETHER A WINE IS STILL GOOD.**

  Both white and red wines turn brown when they finally succumb to oxidation. Whites darken as they age, and red wines fade, slowly losing the color compounds that bond into particles and settle in the bottle as sediment. When you want to know whether a very old bottle may still be good, look at the color. When held up to bright light, does the liquid look dull brown or cloudy? If so, chances are the wine is past its prime. If a red wine still has a red hue or if a white has a golden cast, you may be in luck. Once the bottle is opened and poured, look again. Brownish may be fine, but pure brown is bad news, unless you're drinking Sherry.

- **THE BEST WAY TO FIND OUT IS TO OPEN THE BOTTLE AND TRY IT, BUT IT'S A GOOD IDEA TO HAVE A BACK-UP PLAN.**

  People often feel like they should save mature wines for a special occasion. Unfortunately, far too many are held past their prime. Wine is made to be enjoyed, and the reality is that any day you have a chance to sit down to a meal with loved ones is an occasion to celebrate. So pull out that dusty bottle and try it. A few words to the wise, though. First, mature wines are delicate and will taste better with salty foods than sweet items. A simple cheese plate may be best for the very oldest wines. Second, make sure you have a "Plan B" bottle. The older the wine, the more likely it is to be shot. If you find no pleasure in it, if the flavors fall flat on the palate rather than resonating, you'll feel much better if you have another option.

MARNIE'S CORNER

Wines that will age gracefully for decades are becoming rarer every year. To benefit from long-term bottle aging, a wine must be of high quality and high in components that resist oxidation, such as antioxidant tannins, residual sugar, or natural acidity. The required concentration and balance are not found in modest everyday wines, which are engineered to taste best the day they're purchased. Even among high-quality wines, the modern market demands that they taste great immediately. The traditional techniques that produce long-lived wines, including Barolo and Bordeaux, result in wines that can seem lean or harsh in youth. Even in such regions, winemakers are adjusting their styles to require less patience, to be softer and friendlier on release. The inevitable result is wines that do not age as well in the long term. But since most people would prefer to drink their wine sooner rather than later, this is a good thing overall.

Index

A

acetic acid, 57, 163
acidity, 46, 55, 57–60, 87–88, 123
advice, 78–79, 133, 139, 144–47
aging, 86–89, 168
   barrel aging, 89
   color, 183
   dryness, 55
   longevity, 67
   old wines, 181–84
   oxidation, 183, 184
   spoiled wines, 158
   wine cellars, 182
Albariño, 63, 113
alcohol levels, 13–15, 53
   body and flavor, 21, 62, 75
   grape ripeness, 26
   label information, 82–83
   pairing wine with food, 107,
      109–10, 126–27
   texture, 45
Alsace, 101
American oak, 34–35
anthocyanins, 88
antioxidants, 18, 65–67
appellations, 30
argon, 164
aroma, 49–52
   See also flavor
artichokes, 122–23
asparagus, 122–23
Asti, 116, 179
astringency, 65
   See also tannins
Auslese, 59

B

bad wine, 69–71, 91, 156–59
bag-in-the-box wines, 92–93
Barbera, 59, 96
bargain wines, 94–97
Barolo, 59, 184
barrels, 32–35
barrel toast, 35
Beaujolais, 67, 96, 149
Beerenauslese, 130
Betts, Richard, 44
body, 21–22, 45, 61–64
Bordeaux, 99

acidity, 59
aging, 184
   pairing food with, 122
   tannins, 67
Boru, Olivia, 81
Botrytis cinerea, 130
bouquet, 87–89
boxed wines, 92–93
Brachetto, 96, 116, 179
breathing, 163
brown oak, 34–35
Brunello, 122
Burgundy, 59, 99, 155

C

Cabernet Sauvignon
   acidity, 59
   aging potential, 88
   aroma, 50
   barrel maturation, 33
   body/style, 22, 63
   classics, 99
   pairing food with, 116, 122,
      127, 153
   serving temperature, 169
   tannins, 67–68
   value and price, 95
California, 99
canned wines, 92–93
Caparoso, Randy, 148
capsaicin, 125
carbonation, 13, 55, 179
Cava, 59, 179
cellaring. *See* aging
Chablis, 23, 30
Champagne-style wines, 179
   acidity, 59, 60
   as an aperitif, 153, 177
   carbonation, 13, 55, 179
   chilling, 177–78
      glasses for (flutes), 172
   grapes for, 17
   opening the bottle, 177–79
   pairing food with, 104, 110,
      150, 177
   short-term storage, 168
   sweetness, 55
Chardonnay
   acidity, 59

aging potential, 88
   barrel maturation, 33
   body/style, 22, 63
   classics, 99
   grapes for, 17, 21, 39
   pairing food with, 106, 113,
      122–23, 149
   popularity, 20
   ripeness of grapes in, 23
   sweetness, 55
Chenin Blanc, 96
   acidity, 59
   aging potential, 88
   body/style, 22
Chianti, 59, 60, 153
choosing a wine. *See* restaurant
   wines; shopping for wine
classic wines, 98–101
climate
   New World wines, 40
   old world wines, 39
   ripeness of grapes, 23–27, 58,
      62–63
color of wine, 17–19, 67, 183
cooking with wine, 174–76
cool climates, 26–27
cooperage, 34
corked wines, 91, 157, 159
corks, 84, 90–93, 140
cost of wines, 74–75, 87
   finding values, 75, 94–97
   in restaurants, 139, 146
Curtis, Charles, 177
cyanin, 122–23

D

Dame, Fred, 139
dessert wine, 16, 62, 97
   acidity, 59
   assessing quality, 70
   Botrytis cinerea, 130
   fortified wine, 131
   frozen grape wine, 130
   pairing food with, 116, 128–31,
      150
   sun-dried grape wine, 131
Dexheimer, Fred, 112
Dolcetto, 88
dryness, 13, 15–16, 53–56

Dufault, Christie, 152
Dutton, Traci, 69

E
Edwards, Ron, 94
esters, 50, 87

F
fermentation, 12–14, 26, 53, 58
finesse, 27, 40
finish, 45, 46, 71
flavor
  acidity, 57–60
  aging, 87
  aromas, 49–52
  body, 21–22, 61–64
  bouquet, 87–89
  complexity, 39–40
finesse, 27, 40
fruitiness, 40–41, 87
  nuttiness, 131
  oakiness, 33, 113
  Old vs. New World wines, 36–41
  sweetness and dryness, 13,
    15–16, 53–56
  terroir, 28–31, 36
  umami, 49, 117–20
    See also pairing wine
      with food
flutes, 172
food. See pairing wine with food
fortified wines, 96–97, 131
France, 98–101
freezing wine, 164, 168
French oak, 34–35
Frost, Doug, 117
frozen-grape wine. See Icewine
fruitiness, 40–41, 87
full-bodied wine, 62–64, 149, 163
Fumé Blanc, 59

G
Gallo, Gina, 17
Gamay, 22, 88
gas-preservation systems, 164
Germany, 101
glass bottles, 84, 92–93
glass marbles, 165
glass stoppers, 91
Goldstein, Evan, 104
good wine, 69–71
Grahm, Randall, 36
grape juice, 12–14
grape skins, 17–18, 65–67, 87–88

grape varieties, 20–22, 39, 75–76,
    96
great terroirs, 30
great wines, 71
Grenache, 88, 96, 114–15
Grüner Veltliner, 88, 113, 123, 153

H
heavy wines. See full-bodied wine
home. See serving wine at home
hot foods, 125–27

I
ice, 169
Icewine, 59, 116, 129, 130
inert gas preservation systems, 164
intensity, 107, 153

K
Kacher, Robert, 77

L
labels, 11, 81–85
  grape names, 75–76
  information, 72, 75–76
  modern labels, 83–84
  regional appellations, 30
  traditional labels, 82, 84
lactic acid, 57
late-harvest wines, 129–30
Le Dû, Jean-Luc, 28
left-over wine, 174–76
light-bodied wine, 62–64, 103
  pairing food with, 108–11,
    127, 149
  preserving opened wine, 163
  versatility, 149, 153
Loire Valley, 99–101
Long, Zelma, 65
long-lived wines. See aging

M
Maclean, Natalie, 121
Madeira, 59, 114–15, 176
making wine
  alcohol level, 13–15, 53
  barrel maturation, 32–35
  body, 21–22
  color, 17–19
  dryness and sweetness, 15–16,
    55
  fermentation, 12–15, 53
  grape ripeness, 23–27, 58
  grape varieties, 20–22

old world wines, 39
  temperature, 18
Malbec, 116, 127, 149
Maniec, Laura, 23
marbles, 165
marinades, 175
Marsala, 114–15
Martini, Michael, 180
Mataro grapes, 39
maturation. See aging
medium-bodied wine, 62, 104, 155
medium sweet wine, 16
Médoc district, 99
Merlot
  acidity, 59
  aging potential, 88
  aroma, 50
  body/style, 22
  classics, 99
  grapes for, 39
  pairing food with, 149, 155
microwaving, 169
Mondavi, Michael, 20
monosodium glutamate (MSG),
    118
Monosoff, Melissa, 90
Moscato, 179
mouthfeel, 62, 65, 88
multicourse meals, 148–51
Muscat, 59

N
Nebbiolo, 63, 88
New World wines, 36–41
New Zealand, 101
nitrogen, 164
Noble, Ann C., 49
noble rot, 130
nuttiness, 131

O
oak barrels, 32–35, 113
off-dry wine, 16, 54
Oldman, Mark, 134
old wines. See aging
old world wines, 36–41
olfactory sense. See smell
"on-the-rocks," 169
Oregon, 99
oxidation, 158, 163, 183

P
packaging, 84–85, 90–93
pairing wine with food, 103–7

acidity, 123
alcohol levels, 109–10, 126–27
color matching, 112–16
dessert wines, 128–31
flexible wines, 104
full-bodied wines, 64
light-bodied wines, 108–11, 127
multicourse meals, 148–51
saltiness, 59–60
seasonings and spiciness,
    106–7, 125–27
single-dish pairings, 105–7
sun-dried grapes, 131
umami, 117–20
vegetables, 121–24
weight and intensity, 107, 153
See also restaurant wines
Pedro Ximinez sherry, 116
Pépin, Jacques, 174
Petite Sirah, 59
phenolics, 65–66, 87, 88
pink rosé. *See* rosé wine
Pinot Grigio/Gris
    acidity, 59
    aging potential, 88
    body/style, 22, 63
    grapes for, 17, 21
pairing food with, 113, 122, 149,
    155
Pinot Noir
    acidity, 58, 59
    aging potential, 88
    appearance, 45
    body/style, 22
    classics, 99
    grapes for, 17
pairing food with, 110, 114–15,
    149, 153
poaching, 176
Pomerol district, 99
Port, 59, 116, 131
power, 27
preserving opened wine, 162–65
price. *See* cost of wines
Prosecco, 59, 153, 179

Q
quality, 63, 69–71

R
Ramey, David, 61
recommendations. *See* advice
recycling, 92
red wine, 17–19

aging, 88, 183
antioxidants, 18
appearance, 45
assessing quality, 70
barrel maturation, 33–34
fermentation temperature, 18
flavor, 19
grape skin color, 17–18, 67
multicourse meals, 149
serving temperature, 166–69
tannins, 16, 19, 46, 57, 65–68,
    87–88, 119
umami, 119
refrigeration, 163, 168, 169
regions, 96
    classic (Old World) wines,
        36–41, 98–101
    New World wines, 36–41
    terroir, 28–31, 36
rejecting wines, 91, 156–59
residual sugar, 62
restaurant wines, 133–38
    approving the wine, 140–43,
        156–57
    expert advice, 133, 139, 144–47
    for large groups, 152–55
    multicourse dining, 148–51
    preordering, 148–49
    price, 139, 146
    rejecting a wine, 156–59
    service, 142–43
    sommeliers, 144–46
    wine cabinets, 138
    wine lists, 134–38
Riesling, 96, 101
    acidity, 59
    aging potential, 88
    barrel maturation, 33–34
    body/style, 22, 63
    grapes for, 21
    pairing food with, 110, 113, 127,
        150, 153
    sweetness, 55
Rioja, 59
ripeness of grapes, 23–27, 40
    acidity, 58
    alcohol levels, 26
    body, 62–63
    climate, 23–27, 58
Robinson, Jancis, 86
rosé wine
    aging, 88
    grape skin content, 18
    pairing food with, 113–14, 127,

150, 153

S
salads, 121–22
saltiness, 59
Sancerre, 60
Sangiovese, 21, 22, 88
sautéing, 176
Sauternes, 54
    acidity, 59
    Botrytis cinerea, 130
    pairing food with, 116, 129, 150
Sauvignon Blanc
    acidity, 59
    aging potential, 88
    body/style, 22, 63
    classics, 99–101
    pairing food with, 106, 113,
        122–23, 149, 153
Sbragia, Ed, 12
scents, 45, 49–52, 87–89
    See also flavor
scores, 79
screw tops, 84, 90–93, 159
secondary scents, 87–89
sediment, 88
Selvaggio, Piero, 156
Semillon, 88
serving temperature, 59, 166–69
serving wine at home, 161
    choosing wineglasses, 170–73
    cooking with wine, 174–76
    freshness, 161
    long-term storage, 167–68
    preserving opened wine, 162–65
    temperature of wine, 166–69
Sherry, 96–97
    acidity, 59
    cooking with, 176
    pairing food with, 116, 131
Shiraz/Syrah
    acidity, 59
    aging potential, 88
    appearance, 45
    barrel maturation, 33
    body/style, 22, 63
    grapes, 39
    pairing food with, 116, 122, 155
    popularity, 20
    tannins, 68
shopping for wine, 72–76
    advice and recommendations,
        78–79
    aging considerations, 86–89

alcohol levels, 82–83
    classic wines, 98–101
    corks and tops, 84, 90–93
    finding values, 75, 94–97
    labels, 72, 75–76, 81–85
    packaging, 84–85, 90–93
    price, 74–75, 87
    where to shop, 77–80
    wine scores, 79
skins. *See* grape skins
smell, 45, 47, 49–52, 87–89
    See also flavor
sniffing, 45
Soave, 96
sommeliers, 144–46
sparging, 164
sparkling wine, 179
    as an aperitif, 154, 177
    assessing quality, 70
    carbonation, 13, 55, 180
    chilling, 177–78
    glasses for (flutes), 172
    Italian reds, 96
    multicourse meals, 149
    opening the bottle, 177–79
    pairing food with, 127, 150,
        153, 177
    preserving opened wine, 163
    See also Champagne-style wines
spicy foods, 125–27
spoiled wine, 70, 91, 156–59
Squires, Mark, 166
St. Emilion district, 99
stainless-steel tanks, 33, 34
stelvin screwtops, 91–92
stemware, 142, 170–73
Stevenson, Tom, 32
Stone, Larry, 144
stores, 77–80
storing wines, 166–69
Stout, Guy, 125
sugar. *See* alcohol; sweetness
sun-dried grapes, 131
sunshine. *See* climate
sweetness, 13, 15–16, 53–56
    See also dessert wine
synthetic corks, 91, 159

T

tannins, 16, 19, 46, 57, 65–68
    aging, 87–88, 184
    mouthfeel, 65–66
    from oak, 32, 34
    umami's impact on, 119

tartness. *See* acidity
taste. *See* flavor
taste buds, 49, 117–18
tasting wine, 43–48
    acidity, 57–60
    amplifying sensations, 48
    appearance, 45
    assessing quality, 69–71
    body, 61–64
    describing the aroma, 49–52
    finish, 45, 46, 71
    sweetness/dryness, 53–56
    swirling and sniffing, 45, 47, 62,
        140–43
    swishing and spitting, 46
    tannins, 46, 57, 65–68
    See also flavor
tears, 62
technological innovation, 36, 37
temperature
    acidity, 59
    fermentation, 18
    New World wines, 40
    Old World wines, 39
    ripeness of grapes, 23–27, 58
    for serving and drinking, 166–69
Tempranillo, 88
terroir, 28–31, 36
texture, 45, 46, 61
    See also body
Theise, Terry, 108
thick glass bottles, 84
Thomas, Tara Q., 170
toast, 35, 113
Tokaji Aszu, 59, 116, 130
Torrontes, 96
Triffon, Madeline, 73
Trimbach, Jean, 53

U

umami, 49, 117–20
UV rays, 84, 92

V

vacuum pumps, 164
value, 75, 94–97
varietals, 20–22, 96
vegetables, 121–24
Verdicchio, 122–23
Vernaccia, 122–23
versatility, 153
vinegar, 70, 123, 158, 163
Vinho Verde, 110, 155
Vin Santo, 59, 129, 131

Viognier
    acidity, 59
    aging potential, 88
    body/style, 22, 63
    pairing food with, 113
viscosity, 45, 62
Vitis vinifera, 20
Vouvray, 54

W

warm climates, 26–27
weather. *See* climate
weight, 107, 153
Weiss, Michael, 57
white oak, 34–35
white wine, 17–19
    acidity, 88
    aging, 88, 183
    appearance, 45
    assessing quality, 70
    barrel maturation, 33–34
    fermentation temperature, 18
    grape color, 17–18
    pairing food with, 110, 121–24,
        127, 149
    serving temperature, 166–69
    versatility, 149
Wiegand, Ronn, 162
wine cellars, 166–68, 182
wineglasses, 142, 170–73
wine stores, 77–80
wooden barrels, 32–35

Y

yeasts, 12–14

Z

Zinfandel, 96
    acidity, 58, 59
    aging potential, 88
    body/style, 63
    grapes for, 21, 39
    pairing food with, 106, 127, 155
Ziraldo, Don, 128
Zraly, Kevin, 98

Acknowledgments

I would like to express my deepest thanks to the forty experts who contributed to this book. I was humbled by their generosity and will never forget their support. I am also grateful to the team at Quirk Books for all their assistance.

About the Author

MARNIE OLD SERVED AS DIRECTOR OF WINE STUDIES OF MANHATTAN'S RENOWNED FRENCH CULINARY INSTITUTE. SHE IS ONE OF THE COUNTRY'S TOP SOMMELIERS, recognized for her energetic performance style, intuitive explanations, and common-sense approach to complex wine topics. Marnie is host of *Uncorked*, a weekly wine webisode series at philly.com, as well as a contributing editor for *Santé* magazine and the drinks columnist for *Philadelphia* magazine. Her first book, *He Said Beer, She Said Wine*, is a lively and entertaining debate on food pairing, with coauthor Sam Calagione, founder of Dogfish Head Craft Brewery.

Marnie has earned expert-level credentials from internationally recognized organizations; she has passed the Court of Master Sommeliers' rigorous Advanced Sommelier exams and has earned the respected Advanced Certificate from the Wine & Spirits Education Trust. She served as founding education chair of the American Sommelier Association and has taught award-winning wine classes to both consumers and her industry peers since 1998.

In 2001, Marnie launched her independent consulting, entertaining, and education venture, Old Wines, LLC, becoming one of the country's few independent wine professionals. A native of Winnipeg, Canada, she currently lives and works near Independence Hall, in the heart of historic Philadelphia.

irreference \ir-'ef-(ə-)rən(t)s\ *n* (2009)

1 : irreverent reference

2 : real information that also entertains or amuses

How-Tos. Quizzes. Instructions.
Recipes. Crafts. Jokes.
Trivia. Games. Tricks.
Quotes. Advice. Tips.

Learn something. Or not.

VISIT IRREFERENCE.COM
The New Quirk Books Web Site